Debonico Aleski Brandy-Williams hails from the British Virgin Islands, but spent his formative years growing up in the beautiful Caribbean island of Saint Christopher and Nevis, more commonly known as Saint Kitts and Nevis. He is the third of six siblings from a single parent household. Debonico, or Aleski, as he is more widely known by, is quite vocal and unapologetic on social issues that he is passionate about, and is not afraid to use his voice, verbal or written, to fight for and stand up for what is right and for what is fair. Aleski holds a BSc in Criminology and Youth Studies from London Metropolitan University, and a MA in social work from Middlesex University in London, United Kingdom.

Debonico Aleski
Brandy-Williams

MY JOURNEY TO BECOMING A BLACK MALE SOCIAL WORKER

Challenges, Reflections and Lived Experiences

AUSTIN MACAULEY PUBLISHERS™

LONDON · CAMBRIDGE · NEW YORK · SHARJAH

A CIP catalogue record for this title is available from the British Library.

ISBN 9781398459960 (Paperback)
ISBN 9781398459977 (ePub e-book)

www.austinmacauley.com

First Published 2022
Austin Macauley Publishers Ltd®
1 Canada Square
Canary Wharf
London
E14 5AA

I would like to express my gratitude to everyone who gave me their support, guidance, and encouragement since the start of my social work journey, to where I am today. Without you, I would not be where I am today and my journey would not have been successful.

Some of you were my mentors, my advisers, and interview subjects. A few of you even read my drafts and suggested edits, and for this I will be eternally grateful. There were times when I did not believe in myself, but you believed in me and gave me the motivation to go on.

When I was in my darkest moments, the light of your kindness, generosity, love, and friendship guided me and comforted me. Some of you fed me, clothed me, and even protected me from myself. You brought me out of my depression by illuminating my path.

I am grateful for the many telephone calls, texts, and visits to simply check on me. I appreciate the extended deadlines and the further reading recommendations. I valued the time off you gave me so that I could rest, rejuvenate, and take care of myself. You saw that I needed it and you gave it to me without me having to ask.

You took time out of your busy day to mentor me, made sure I understood the processes and procedures and reminded me to always be vigilant. You used your past experiences and future aspirations to inspire me. You made me want to be the best that I could be.

I am Debonico Aleski Brandy-Williams, a qualified social worker and I owe it all to you!
Thank you!

Table of Contents

Foreword One

I'm honoured to write this foreword for Debonico Aleski Brandy-Williams' book, *My Journey to Becoming a Black Male Social Worker*. I became aware of Aleski in 2019, when he sent me a copy of his dissertation on the experiences of black male social workers called *The Black Male Effect: Challenges & Experiences of Young Black Male Social Workers in Children and Young People Services.*

I remember being amazed by the accuracy and authenticity of his scholarship. Unsurprisingly, much of his dissertation conveyed my own professional challenges and lived experiences. Aleski kindly agreed to let me add his dissertation to my repository to share with my networks. It is something I often share with people to highlight the hidden and suppressed narratives of black male social workers.

I'm confident that the experiences Aleski captures in his dissertation and this book will firmly resonate with many black male social workers. Furthermore, my own experiences captured in *Ambition Navigation* in the anthology, *OUTLANDERS: Hidden Narratives from Social Workers of Colour* and other chapters of that book, showcase a rich and diverse collection of essays, poems, stories and reflections, providing unique and spellbinding insights from social workers of colour.

I hope that Aleski's book will be considered as another valuable resource to educate, empower, and equip all social workers from all backgrounds in policy, practice, and education for decades to come.

'One world, one race... the human race!'

Wayne Reid
@wayne_reid79
@BASW_UK
#CrushingStereotypesDaily

Foreword Two

Debonico Aleski Brandy-Williams is a bit of a rarity. As a black male social worker, he's a minority in a minority. Statistics from the gov.uk website tell us that on 30 September 2020, there were 31,854 children and family social workers in England and the 'overwhelming majority' of those social workers, 86%, were female. (https://explore-education-statistics.service.gov.uk/find-statistics/children-s-social-work-workforce).

In terms of ethnicity, the most recent data available, again from the UK government website, indicates that just 11.1% of children and family social workers in England are black (https://www.ethnicity-facts-figures.service.gov.uk/workforce-and-business/workforce-diversity/social-workers-for-children-and-families/latest#:~:text=71.7%25%20of%20child%20and%20family,Caribbean%20and%201.9%25%20Other%20Black).

So, there really aren't many out there like Aleski, and for me, that's just one of the reasons why this book is so important. We don't hear much from black male social workers, and so to be able to write a foreword for one in this much-needed book, is a real pleasure for me.

This book is a warts-and-all telling of the experiences of a black man navigating the complex world of social work from training to post-qualifying. It's a journey that I'm sure you will find a real eye-opener regardless of whether you share similar characteristics to Aleski or not.

Students, lecturers, and social workers from all ethnic backgrounds should all read this book.

Students – you'll realise that the challenges you face as you pursue your studies are not necessarily unusual and *can* be overcome!

Lecturers and qualified social workers/managers – this book will be a timely reminder of some of the pressures and additional hardships that black students are having to manage as they complete their education, and find their place in the world of qualified social work.

The book will also be reminder to all of the amazing things that can be achieved when a listening ear, support, and when needed, going the extra mile, can bring about.

To all the black male students (and qualified) social workers reading this – no one said it would be easy, but dig deep and hang in there.

There is much to learn on the journey – read on to find out!

Diane Apeah-Kubi
Senior Lecturer, Social Work
@DAKubi

Prelude – University Years

'Non Multa, Sed Multum'

That was the motto for my old secondary school back in the Caribbean. It can be translated many ways, but for us at secondary school, it meant 'Not quantity, but quality'. This motto was embedded into the ethos of the school and intertwined into the morals and values we were taught. The Latin words and their translation was also mentioned in the official school song.

Not quantity, but quality. This is how I feel about my two years attending Middlesex University (MDX). It also remains how I feel about the post-graduation degree I still enjoy with the university as an institution, and the staff members I still communicate with. Since graduating in August 2019, I have had the opportunity to mentor and support social worker students and join in on several Zoom sessions to share snippets of my journey with them.

I sometimes reflect on my time at MDX and frankly, I would not change a thing about it. There was a time in my second year where I felt unsupported but it made me a better person personally, and a better social worker professionally.

These moments of doubt and the context around them will be discussed in detail in the early chapters of this book.

The thing I enjoyed about MDX, was its open and inclusive approach to learning and promoting individual thinking. There was one tutor who kept reminding us that we are Masters' students and thus should not solely rely on lectures and seminars for information and knowledge. She said that we should be researching before and after each lecture and seminar so that we can respectfully challenge the lecturers and seminar leaders.

At that time, I must admit, a lot of us students thought that this lecture was simply trying to abdicate her duties and responsibilities. We discussed it among ourselves abs concluded that we paid for lectures abs seminars so we should have the full benefit of each. Further, we thought that since we were relatively new to social work, we needed as much guidance and support as possible.

What we didn't realise at that time was that this lecturer was quietly preparing us for what lies ahead. She was in essence, moulding us into forward-thinking social workers who were able to make independent and informed interventions and decisions in the best interest of the children and their families. I am sure my fellow students would agree with me here on what I am about to say next.

As much as you are part of a team when you start working after leaving university, social work is a very solitary job. You visit families alone most times, you attend meetings and conferences alone most times, you undertake assessments and write reports alone most times, and you alone make recommendations on interventions most times.

Even though you would have supervision with your line manager, you are required to be able to defend your decisions and explain how you arrived at those decisions. So, asking us to undertake individual and independent study and research was not such a bad thing after all.

Another thing that I thoroughly enjoyed about how the social work course is structured, is that every other week the undergraduate and postgraduate students would come together for a couple of lectures. One of them being on the Law module. I found this very helpful and informative as it allowed me to hear how the law was being understood and interpreted by others. I would even go as far as to say that in my opinion, the undergraduate students had a better grasp than me on the law as it relates to social work.

The university also has a fantastic teaching partnership with many local authorities, and this benefited me tremendously as a student social worker. We would have lectures and seminars being led by senior management social workers from these local authorities.

They would give presentations and case studies on the work their respective teams were undertaking and the work they had done with children and families. I paid keen attention as I was thoroughly fascinated with the complexities of their work and the successful outcomes they achieved.

I also liked the fact that these visiting professionals did not just paint a rosy picture of social work. That gave a balanced view and I think the university insisted on this. During these lectures and seminars, I heard how social workers were verbally and physically abused, how some left the job due to stress-related illnesses, and how some were not as diligent in their duties as they should have been. Some of these accounts scared me a little, but I was still passionate about becoming a social worker.

I remember when I applied and was accepted to MDX, I had to attend several open and information evenings. This was a chance for us to meet with the teaching team and also to meet with fellow students. At one of these information evenings, one of the teaching team asked a very simple but serious question. She asked, by show of hands, how many of us wanted to be social workers. And as you can guess, all of us raised our hands. She smiled and left it there.

At the end of the information evenings, after we had been given a glimpse into what the course entails and what life as a social worker can potentially be like, the same member of the teaching team came back and stood in front of the group. Again, she asked us, by show of hands, how many of us still really wanted to be social workers.

This time, only three-quarters of the hands went up. Some expressed doubt about whether or not this career choice was for them after what they had heard that night. When we eventually started attending lectures and seminars, lots of the faces I had seen at the information evenings were nowhere to be found.

MDX taught me that if you are not passionate about something, you will not be able to give it your best, especially through challenging times. At every point in my two years at MDX, we were reminded about the good that we can do as social workers, and the bad that can happen to us. Most of the bad had to do with the unpredictability of the families we would be working with.

Although I would not change anything about my experience at Middlesex University, I would however like to make one suggestion. I think that once the students know where they would be undertaking their placements, a representative from there should come to the university and facilitate a session in processes, procedures, and what to expect.

This session should also include the students been shown blank templates of the forms and online episodes they would be required to complete. An introduction to the Case Management system used can also be included in this session.

The reasons why I say this is solely based on my experience as a student social worker and as some who supported and supervised students on their placements. It can be a daunting and overwhelming feeling at the start of placements when you're just sat there trying to get on with tasks. Quite often, you see the social workers getting on with their work and you feel as if you would be disturbing them by asking them questions. I know students should not feel like that but the reality is that it happens.

I can't end without mentioning the awesome and great friends I met at MDX. These were fellow students on my course and others I met at the library or chilling in the quad. You see, Middlesex University promotes a balance experience and encouraged students to have some fun as well. It's a holistic experience and environment. One that I dear missed but will always remember.

Here is my ode to Middlesex University:

For a life of public service, you have prepared me
You reminded me how to think independently
You took the best of me and moulded me
Into the social worker, I was destined to be

You taught me the values that I should live by
You pushed me to reach unknown levels up high
I'm soaring to heights previously unseen
That's how valuable your guidance has been
I'm ever so grateful for the difference you've made
My respect for you will never fade
I vow to continue being the best that I can be
So, many thanks to my Alma Mater – Middlesex University.

Memorable Moment #1

During my first year at university, I decided to put my name forward to be Student Voice Leader for our cohort. This decision came after I was in a class, with the other students, and another lecturer opened the door and rudely interrupted the class. It seems as though there was a mix-up with the scheduling of rooms, and the room we were in was double booked.

Rather than contacting room bookings, the interrupting lecturer stood at the front of the class and was trying to start an argument with our lecturer. She was also demanding that we leave the room so that her students can come in. Our lecturer was trying to advise her that our class was booked for the room for the next 45 minutes and she wanted to continue.

We, the students, also stood our ground and insisted that the interrupting lecturer leave the room so that our class can continue. She eventually did but was stood outside the door with daggers in her eyes.

At the student elections, I was elected Student Voice Leader and attended meetings with the course leaders and also module leaders. In these meetings, I brought forward the concerns and issues that were raised by my fellow students and suggested possible remedies and outcomes. I also had many meetings with the students so that I can give them feedback on what was discussed at the meetings.

Being a Student Voice Leader also gave me the chance to further develop my leadership and organisational skills. I advocated on their behalf and represented their best interest at meetings. During my tenure as Student Voice Leader, there were some improvements on some issues. One issue that was resolved was that of advance notifications of room bookings. This was because, on some occasions, students were not advised of what rooms we would be in until the morning of the class.

I did not continue as Student Voice Leader into my second and final year as I wanted to focus more on my dissertation research project. We were not having classes often as we were on the 100-day placements. I hope that my tenure and work undertaken as Student Voice Leader was as beneficial to my fellow students as it was for me. This period stands as another of my memorable moments.

Chapter One – First Placement

It was the first day of my 70-day placement, and to be honest, I remembered I was so nervous. I felt as if I was a sacrificial lamb being sent to the slaughter. Having no idea of what to expect going into a new venture is always daunting. All sorts of thoughts about what could go wrong were swirling around my head. In my mind, it was all going to go horribly wrong and my first day could very well be my last day.

Reflecting back now, I can appreciate how ill-prepared I was for my first social work placement. There was no preparation or guidance from my university on what to expect. There were no placement scenarios given, no examples of the work to be undertaken, and no information given on the specific teams or departments I had been placed in. All I was told was to research the local authority before attending on my first day.

Don't get me wrong, I learnt a lot from university. However, in my opinion, it was all surface level with no real depth. Sure, we learnt about social work theories, the stages of child development, the use of self in social work, and how to undertake research, and that was about it. Oh, and we also learnt the difference between adult social work and social work with children and families. We skimmed over mental health definitions and thresholds for hospital admissions, we briefly touched on the law as it relates to social work and we did a few case studies and one role play.

The only practical exercise that we did was an 8–10-week child observation. We, the students, had to find a nursery or childcare provider who would allow us to undertake a fly-on-the-wall observation of a child five years of age and below. With the consent of the parents, we had to observe and analyse that child's every move one day per week for 10 weeks. Then back at university we discussed it and completed an assignment on it. This was for us to understand the stages of child development and see the subtle changes in the child's behaviour and growth.

However, for me as a young black male social worker, this exercise did not sit well with me and I brought this up in group discussions and also mentioned it in my assignment submission. For lack of a better word, I felt like a pervert following around a young child, not interacting with them, not making it obvious that I was observing them but just stealthily and nonchalantly stalking them. It was a horrendous experience and I was only too happy when it was over.

Having gone through that unpleasant experience, imagine my utter shock and surprise when during my first placement I was told by a service manager that that exercise was a waste of time as social workers do not evaluate or analyse the stages of child development. That is left up to the Midwives, Health Visitors, and School Nurses who provide social workers with reports and attend meetings to expound on those reports. Well, you could have knocked me over with a feather.

At university, we spent a vast amount of time dissecting social work theories from every conceivable angle. We research the theorists, their methods, their studies, their supporters and critiques, and aspects of their known personal lives. And we were advised and encouraged to know these theories inside and out as we would have to include them in all our reports – at the local authority level and also at court proceedings. In essence, we were to live, breathe and embrace theories and we did just that.

However, and it's a huge however. The first week of my first placement I was actively discouraged from using theories in any of my written and oral reports. I was flabbergasted. It just did not make any sense to me so of course, I had to ask why. I was told that using theories in my work would open me up to being challenged from all angles and my professional judgement being questioned.

You see, theories are subjective and can be interpreted in many ways, and can be used to both support and argue against cases or court orders. Further, theories are dispelled all the time and new research and counter theories are being developed all the time. Thus, to stake your recommendations or conclusions on a theory can be the beginning of the end of one's career. I kid you not.

At university, they don't fully prepare you for what can go wrong either. And I'm not talking about putting case notes in the wrong file or going to the wrong address, I'm talking about more serious things. Like complaints being made against you from clients. They call it an allegation against a professional. This happened to me in my very first placement and threw me for a loop. I broke down and cried to my Team Manager and Deputy Team Manager. Let me tell you what happened.

I was allocated a case of a young man who had behavioural issues and his parents were finding it difficult to deal with him. I went in, spoke to him and his parents and we agreed on some intervention methods and strategies (my background in Youth Work helped here) which worked for a while.

However, something happened at the school that triggered him and his behaviour escalated to the point where the threshold for taking the case to an Initial Child Protection Conference (ICPC) was met so I initiated the process after discussing it with the parents and they agreed and understood. Or so I thought.

The next thing I know, a few days later, the mother called my deputy team manager and alleged all sorts against me. Oh, my word. An investigation then ensued and I was placed on restrictive duties and my placement tutor from my university was informed. I had meetings after meetings while the investigations were ongoing to the point where it stressed me out, made me think that my social work career was over before it had even started.

I remembered the day when my Deputy Manager saw that this incident was taking a toll on me and called me into a side office where I broke down and cried my eyes out. She was so supportive and just held me and allowed me to cry then compose myself. I will always remember her for that. Even to this day, I keep in contact with her.

The allegations were found to be malicious and the case was closed. The parents were upset that the case was being escalated and thought that if they make false allegations against me that the case was escalation would not proceed.

During the investigations, my placement tutor was also very supportive and offered me extra support and time away from classes. The same can't be said for the course leaders who simply brushed my very traumatic experience away and stated that it was part and parcel of being a social worker. They even used my experience as a 'teaching moment'.

Here I was, a first-year student on my very first placement, having false allegations made against me, stressed out, having a breakdown and none of the course leaders offered any assistance. No counselling was offered, none of them asked me how I felt, none of them asked me how they could help and none of them even showed that they remotely cared.

I was left to fend for myself while my experience was dismissed. If it weren't for my team members at work and my placement tutor, I don't know how I would have even made it to the end of my first placement.

The rest of my first placement went splendidly after that incident as I now had extra knowledge and practical skills and experiences of what it meant to be a social worker. Before my placement ended, I had dealt with young people and families experiencing bereavements, mental health issues, abandonment, a child going missing, being excluded from school, and even one child setting his bedroom on fire.

My team managers, in supervision and team meetings, commented and commended me on my work ethics and case management and gave me cases of various particulars and complexities to work on. This helped with my development as a student and as a social worker.

During my first placement as well, my team managers recognised the good work that I was doing in engaging with young people and gaining their trust and I was asked to undertake some paid mentoring sessions with young people classes as 'hard to reach' or 'difficult to engage with'. That was a bonus to my learning as I was also able to demonstrate my existing skills and knowledge and merge them with the skills and knowledge that I was gaining and developing as a budding social worker.

After my first placement finished, the service manager and team manager offered me a job as a social work assistant (SWA) while on break from university. I jumped at that rare opportunity as it would mean me getting more experience and knowledge and a somewhat steady pay-check which was a huge blessing for a full-time student with only student finance as an income – if you can even call student finance an income.

As an SWA, just like the latter days of my first placement, I worked independently and autonomously on cases. These cases were always evaluated and then signed off by the Team Manager or the Deputy Team Manager. Truth be told, I felt like a fully-fledged social worker.

I was undertaking visits, competing Child and Family Assessments (CFA), devising and managing Child in Need (CIN) Plans, and even attended several ICPC with qualified social workers. I was flying high as an SWA and loving every moment. Everything I did and everywhere I went within the local authority I felt like I was a part of a family – a family I always wanted to be a part of.

I had this same feeling during my placement and this led me to ask if I could undertake my second placement within a different team in that same local authority. I was advised that it was highly unusual for a student to do both placements with one employer but the request would be made to see if it was possible.

Oh, you can't imagine the feeling I had when it was confirmed that the university had agreed for me to do my second placement at the LA. I was over the moon... So, it was a seamless transition from being a paid SWA to being an unpaid second placement student.

Chapter Two – Second Placement

My second and final placement was with the Fostering Team and while it was not my first choice, the team manager who 'interviewed' me made me feel as if I had won the lottery in being allocated to her team. She was just amazing and is another mentor that I kept in touch with even after the placement finished. Later on, you will see how she came to mean so much to me, both professionally and personally.

The pace of work in the Fostering Team was quite slower than what I expected and was quite different from that of the localities team. While localities involved visits within twenty-four hours or 10 days or within four weeks, in the Fostering team, visits were much less frequent at once every six to eight weeks and assessments can take up to six months or more.

However, there were open evenings to plan and attend, training days to facilitate for foster carers, and recruitment drives to attract more foster carers. All in all, a comprehensive and steady experience. I got to see what it is like for young people to be in foster care and also better understand the role that foster carers play in shaping young lives. Sometimes there were challenges and difficulties between foster carer and young person, and that is where the fostering team comes in to help manage the situation and prevent a breakdown in the foster placement.

Speaking of placement breakdown, second placement and university journey almost came to an abrupt end when I became homeless. I found out that my landlord was a council tenant and illegally subletting to me. When I notified her that I would be moving out as soon as possible, she stopped responding to any messages or calls to discuss the matter.

However, on New Year's Eve, while I was preparing to have a few friends over, she came to the flat and demanded that I leave immediately. Long story short, the police were called, she made up some falsehoods about me being in the flat without permission and the police asked me to leave.

Even though I provided proof of the lease that was signed and bank statements of me paying the rent each month, the police said that as she was the legal holder of a lease from a local authority, they had no choice but to ask me to leave. I disagreed with their decision but they were adamant that I had to leave or they would arrest me. They gave me just 30 minutes to back a bag or two and advised me to make arrangements to come back within a few days to collect the rest of my belongings. Wow.

That night, I spent about 2-3 hours in a nearby Mcdonald's calling friends asking for a place to crash. However, as it was New Year's Eve – the holidays – all of my friends had family members staying over and thus could not host me. I then started calling budget hotels and motels to see if there was a chance a room was available and I was having no luck.

Just as I was about to give up and resign myself to sleeping rough, the last Premier Inn on my list to call said they had one room available but I could not reserve it. It was on a first come first served basis and cost £191.00 for the night and decreasing by about approximately £20-£30 the next two nights and then to just under £100 on subsequent nights. I begged the receptionist to hold the room for me but she would not budge.

So, I quickly booked an Uber to the Premier Inn over 45 minutes away and prayed that I got there before anyone else. When I got there, I rushed into the reception and my heart sank. There was someone in front of me asking about the room. He was trying to pay for the room with a card and somehow it was not going through.

He asked the receptionist if she can hold the room for him while he goes in search of a cash machine and she told him that she can't. He turned around and looked at me and must have thought that I had a reservation as he pointed to his bag and asked me to keep an eye on it for him. Before I could even reply, he rushed out the door in search of a cash machine.

Now, I had no cash on me and just had my card so I was sure that I would be in the same predicament as him and the card machine would not work. I went up to the desk and asked to book a room. The lady looked at me and it must be my lucky day as there was only one room left and it was available on a first-come-first-served basis.

I told her that I was aware as I was the guy who called her on the phone and was begging her to hold the room for me. She laughed and that it looks like the room was supposed to be mine and then she proceeded to make the booking.

I handed over my driver's license and she entered my details. Then she punched some more keys on the keyboard and then asked if the dreaded question of whether I was paying by cash or card. When I said card, she causally mentioned that that card machine was not working and had been giving some trouble since earlier that day. I asked her if she can try it one more time just to see if it was working and she reluctantly agreed.

She punched in the amount on the card machine and then asked me to enter my card and my pin. I was praying the entire time. My hands were shaking as I put my card into the slot. My feet were trembling as I punched in my pin. My heart was racing as the machine began to process the transaction. Then the door behind me opened and in came the gentleman from earlier with a wad of cash in his hand. My heart stopped beating and I felt faint.

But I was jolted back to life when I heard the sweetest sound ever. A sharp ping and paper scrolling from the card machine followed by surprise laughter from the receptionist. I turned around and she was handing me the receipt and keys to the room. She said that I was blessed. I was so dazed that I could not respond. I smiled, took the keys and receipt, dragged my bag to the lift, and got on.

I was hardly breathing. I got off the lift on the third floor and walked to the room. I opened the door, dragged my bag in, and closed the door. I walked to the bed, sat down, and just broke down and cried like a baby. The emotions that washed over me were powerful and overwhelming. I just cried and cried and cried. Even now, I don't even know how long I cried for.

When I finally composed myself, I took a shower, went and found a shop and bought some food and got back to the room, and just sat there staring out of the window. Then my phone rang. It was my team manager from the Fostering Team. I picked up the phone and said hello.

My team manager said that somehow, I was on her mind and she felt a strong urge to call me. She asked me if I was okay and I could not respond. Once again, I started to cry. She heard me crying and kept asking me what's wrong and if I was okay. Her voice sounded as like it was breaking.

I managed to stop crying long enough to tell her what had happened and where I was at. I was so touched when she started crying and telling me she was so sorry. I think the gravity of the situation was too much for her and she said that she would give me a call back.

When she called me back, she stated that she had to get off the phone as she was too emotional and was crying over my situation. She couldn't believe that on New Year's Eve, I was homeless and in a budget hotel. We talked for a few minutes more and she prayed for me. She told me to get some sleep and that she would check in on me the next day.

Not only did she call me the next day (New Year's Day), and the day after they, she called me every single day for that entire week and gave me the time off for me to go to the council for me to complete a homelessness application and request housing. The following week I moved to Travelodge, which was cheaper than Premier Inn, while I continued to liaise with the council and attend my placement. I spent two full weeks in motels before I was granted temporary housing and placed on the social housing register.

On the first day of university in January 2019, I went to my university to meet with one of the lead lecturers for my course. I explained the situation to her, asked for some time off from attending physical lessons while I try to sort everything out. At that time, I had not been placed in temporary housing as yet. I explained to the lead tutor that I would still work on and complete my assignments and that my dissertation research project would continue and be handed in on time.

Imagine my surprise when she suggested that I should consider withdrawing from university altogether and come back the following academic year... Mind you, I was due to complete my two-year course in May of that year. I only had a couple more assignments to hand in and my dissertation research project was in the final stages.

I just had a few more months to go and all I could get from her was to withdraw and come back the following year. I left her office feeling even worse than I did when I chose to go and see her and explain my situation.

After I left her office, I felt so deflated, so confused and frustrated, and felt that somehow, I was being blamed and unsupported for being homeless. I went to the admissions office and spoke with an advisor who also said that there is nothing they can do and if I miss too many classes then it will count against me and my overall degree classification. Again, I felt let down and felt that the university did not even care about my welfare or how my situation might affect me.

At that point, I gave up completely. I asked the admissions officer to withdraw me from the course. Without saying anything, he punched in some notes on his computer and printed a piece of paper, and handed it to me. He explained that it was my notification of withdrawal and that someone else would call me to speak to me to see if this was what I wanted to do and before the withdrawal was final. I got up and I left.

I called my university tutor and explained the situation to her and bless her, she was so understanding. She asked me to meet her at the university in a few days and I agreed. When we did meet, she was so sympathetic and understanding. She urged me not to withdraw. She reminded me that I was so close to completing.

She reminded me that I was a good student and a good social worker (she never called us student social workers as she believed that once we start placements, we were social workers). She told me that if I had to miss her class then she would gladly give me authorise absences under exceptional circumstances.

Then she did something unexpected, she pulled out her purse and gave me some money (most of my student finance had been spent on the two weeks I spent in budget hotels). I never knew I was so emotional until this situation as once again I broke down and she comforted me. She, my placement tutor, is another of my mentors that I keep in contact with even to this day. She, along with my other mentors, made me into the social worker I am today and this book is dedicated to them all.

After I met with my placement supervisor, I decided not to withdraw but to be strong and carry on. I decided that I would not be beaten by any adversaries or lack of support. I decided that come what may, I was going to finished the race that I started, submit all assignments and my dissertation research project on time and graduate with a distinction. And to accomplish all this, I threw myself completely into academic focus and did not look back.

Chapter Three – Dissertation Research Project

Initially, I wanted to focus my dissertation research project on whether or not social workers hold their close friends and family members to the same exacting standards as they hold their clients. However, I was advised by my Research module lecturer that that topic was too controversial and would potentially paint social workers in a bad light. Further, according to her, it was not an appropriate research area for a social work student. Thus, I went back to the drawing board and had a re-think.

A few days after I was told that my initial topic for my dissertation research project was not going to be approved, I was reminded of an incident that happened during my first placement that would eventually guide the direction of my dissertation research project. Here is what happened.

A young man that I was the allocated social worker for, had a court hearing and he asked me to be there to support him to which I agreed. When I got to the security desk at the court, and before I could say or ask anything, the guard asked me what time was my case listed. I did not think anything of it and thought that it was an innocent mistake that he made thinking that I was a defendant. I showed him my social worker identification and told him that I was there to support one of my young people. He apologised and let me through.

When I got upstairs, I saw the mother of that young person and went to sit next to her. We struck up a conversation about what had happened to her son and what could potentially happen at the court hearing that morning. She was beside herself with worry and I was doing my best to calm her down and reassure her that no matter what happened, I would be there to support her and her son.

While waiting for the case to be called, the court clerk appeared at the entrance of the designated courtroom and scanned the room. Then she made a beeline to me and without asking who I was, she asked me if my solicitor was present. Mind you, at this time I had my social worker identification around my neck, hanging down in front of me in plain sight.

I must have been thrown by her question and did not answer her because she spoke just a little bit louder and again asked me if my solicitor was present. I reached and held up my social worker's identification without saying anything.

She simply looked at it and walked away. No apology, nothing. Her face did it even register any embarrassment or any other emotion to suggest that she was sorry for assuming that I was a defendant in a case. I looked at the mother of my young person and we both just shook our heads in disbelief.

She then pointed out that I was the only black male in the room. I was the only black person in the room, as the mother of my young person was a very light mixed-race lady. We both started to discuss what had just happened and how it was a problem that black men are automatically targeted negatively.

That was probably the very first time that I had observed and experience such direct racial discrimination. There may have been other times in the past but I was oblivious to them.

Having thought of that experience and how it made me feel after the fact, I decided to focus my dissertation research project on the challenges and experiences of young black male social workers. I even came up with a fancy title for it. I officially dubbed it:

The Black Male Effect: Challenges and Experiences of Black Male Social Workers in the Children and Young People Service.

I was pleased as punch with that title and could not wait to get started. I filled in and submitted all the relevant and required documents and sent them off to the Ethics Committee for approval. Once it was approved, I was full steam ahead.

I contacted some black male social workers from across the service and from different Local Authorities and asked them to take part in interviews. All of them consented and shared their varying challenges and experiences. I was both fascinated and shocked by what they told me. I was equally shocked by what I read and researched in preparation for writing my final report.

All through the process, I had fantastic and constant feedback from my wonderful dissertation supervisor. I sent her drafts of the individual sections of my dissertation research project and always received timely and beneficial feedback from her. She suggested books that I could read and referenced, websites that I could peruse, and publications that I could use quotes and excerpts from.

To be honest, I don't think that I could have done it without her supervision. And you guessed it, I still keep in touch with her even up to today. The foreword of this book is written by her and she assisted me with some editing.

In addition to the lived experiences that were shared by the social workers' interviews, I also needed hard data for my dissertation research project. To get this, I decided to send a Freedom of Information request to the Health and Care Professions Council (HCPC), now known as Social Work England, for a list of all social workers in the United Kingdom, their gender, and ethnicity. The information that came back showed that there was a scarcity of males within the profession, especially black male social workers.

I finished up my dissertation research project with all the information received and submitted the final version ahead of schedule. It was a momentous occasion for me as after it was submitted, I felt such a release of tension, anxiety, and stress from my entire body. You have to remember that I was still living in temporary accommodations, bidding every week to secure more permanent housing and trying to plan for my future as a social worker. I felt as if I could not properly plan anything since I was not properly settled.

Luckily, my history with the local authority I was with, placed me in good staring for the first shot at one of their Assisted and Supported Year in Employment (ASYE). I spoke with the Service Manager for the East Locality team and made clear my desire to go back to one of the teams. A few days later I was invited to an interview and subsequently was told that I was successful and offered an ASYE position to start after I had obtained my results from university and had passed.

I did indeed pass with a Distinction and was also singled out for special mention on my dissertation research project and the attention it had received from the British Association of Social Workers (BASW). Let me tell you how this came about and became one of my most celebrated and accomplished achievements.

Chapter Four – My First Official Publication

After I had submitted my dissertation research project to the university to be graded, it was suggested to me that I should look into publishing it as it was an area that had not been properly researched before. I thought about it for a couple of days before I approached BASW to seek some information about being published in the Journal of Social Work.

I was signposted in the right direction but was also asked to submit a copy of my dissertation research project to one of their officers to read. I did that and was surprised when he asked me if I would mind if he shared it with his colleagues and his wider mailing list.

He further stated that it was a very important piece of work that addressed some very important and rarely talked about issues. I told him that I don't mind it being shared with his network and for my contact details to be shared as well.

After he shared it, one of his colleagues contacted me and asked me if I would like to write a viewpoint piece for the Professional Social Work (PSW) magazine. I could not believe it and of course, I said yes. I wrote the piece, sent it to my dissertation supervisor for feedback, and then submitted it to PSW. It was sent back asking for some minor edits and then accepted for publication.

I was too excited to tell anyone and kept it to myself until I was given an advance copy of my article a week before graduation. I sent it to my dissertation supervisor and she stated that she would request that my achievement be recognised and announced during my graduation ceremony. Suffice it to say I was over the moon.

On the day of graduation, when the Head of School gave her speech, she mentioned my name and that my dissertation research project was picked up by my BASW and a viewpoint piece would be published in the next issue of PSW.

I was bursting with pride as the audience cheered loudly and my fellow graduates congratulated me with hugs, kind words, and pats on my back and shoulders. When I went to cross the stage, the Head of School shook my hand and said that she looked forward to reading my dissertation research project and my viewpoint piece in PSW.

I walked back to my seat with a wide grin on my face. With all the challenges and experiences, I had been doing through that past year, I had survived. I made it.

For your reading pleasure, please see below the viewpoint piece I wrote for PSW. Happy reading.

Black men in social work are stereotyped

Aleski Brandy-Williams says black male social workers face unfair challenges that need to be addressed

Being a black male and a social worker is to face stereotyping and unwelcome assumptions. I found this out myself as a student on placement when I was in youth court. Despite wearing a branded lanyard identifying me as a social worker, I was approached by a court official who assumed I was the defendant. I was the only black male in the room.

As a result of this, I focused my social work dissertation on examining the challenges and lived experiences of young black male social workers. I interviewed workers within children's social services. My findings highlighted some uncomfortable truths. Here are some of the themes.

Stereotyping and typecasting: Young black men are more often than not categorised and stereotyped based on their gender and ethnicity. The negative rhetoric perpetuated about young black males in society as being involved in drugs, gangs and crime is partly to blame. As a result, they experience a high level of typecasting in terms of the types of cases they get and the kinds of service users they work with. For example, a repeated theme was an unrealistic and unfounded view and expectation that young black males are better suited and able to work with children, young people and families who are involved in and affected by criminal activity. Almost all the black male social workers I interviewed worked with service users who were either black or from an ethnic minority background.

Under scrutiny: Interviewees expressed frustration about the way they felt their practice, professional conduct and ability to do their job was scrutinised and questioned more than their white colleagues. It seemed to them the solutions and interventions they put forward were dissected more intensely and as a result they were left fighting feelings of inadequacy and incompetence.

Lack of support and training: There was a perception that young black male social workers do not receive the level of support and opportunities for additional training that would help them in advancing their careers into senior and management positions.

> 'A lack of role models in management roles is a vital gap to address'

A number of the interviewees observed the higher up the management ladder they looked, the whiter it became. One interviewee said the lack of black managers in social work made it unlikely for black men to make it into management.

Sell-outs: Young black men can face being labelled as 'sell-outs' in the black community. Some black service users view them as an extension of a racist and discriminatory institution that is out to oppress them. When dealing with black children and families, black men are expected to side with and understand the situations of these families on the basis that they share some of the same ethnicity, culture, background and traditions.

Sexuality and trauma: Another issue that emerged was around stereotypes toward those who go into 'caring professions' such as social work. The black men I interviewed felt there was a question mark put over their sexuality and sexual orientation. Prejudice against sexual orientation has no place in social work and goes against the values of the profession. However, the males I interviewed felt a persistence of such stereotyping still prevents some black men – and men in general – from seeking a career in social work. Another unhelpful assumption black male social workers experienced was that they had some level of trauma in their lives and upbringing which led them into a career in social work. It was felt this assumption was not something imposed as much on their white counterparts.

If we are to get more black males into social work there is work to be done. A vital gap is a lack of role models in management. A chicken and egg situation also exists due to a lack support and training to enable black men – and black social workers generally – to break through into those roles.

If we are to ensure equality of opportunity, I believe my study has important lessons for social work employers. It also has repercussions for the communities we work with in terms of promoting culturally-appropriate practice.

Aleski Brandy-Williams is a newly qualified social worker in children and young people's services

Chapter Five – Case Study Part One

One of my university assignments during placement was to write a case study based on a young person I was the allocated social worker for. Below is one that I submitted which gained me a Grade 2 and awesome feedback from the first and second markers. It is in two parts.

Thyer (2010) states that in social work learning and practice, case studies are an integral part of reflecting on the work that has been done and looking at best practice methods and outcomes in addition to evaluating and guiding how theory is applied to practice. Further, having the knowledge, experience, and ability to develop one's case study for reflective purposes shows that one is taking ownership of one's own professional as well as personal development (Eraut, 2002). This is indeed the purpose of writing and reflecting on this case study. The main aim is to show that as a social work student, I have not only applied the knowledge and theory learnt to my actual practice but also have found ways to tailor such practice to the needs of my allocated service users. This has been and will be demonstrated in the interventions done with the service user, how I have advocated for change or services on behalf of the service user, and the positive outcomes of these interventions and advocacy.

The service user who is the focus of this case study will be called Paulette and she has been an approved Foster Carer for over fifteen years. During that time, she has fostered five young persons on respite, short and long-term placements. Paulette is a 60-year-old black British female who was born in the Caribbean and migrated to the United Kingdom before the age of ten. She has one biological son who lives with his family. Paulette lives alone in a three-bedroom property that she has owned for over 10 years. Currently, she has one 17-year-old male child she is fostering on a long-term basis and has been asked to provide respite for another 15-year-old male child whose current foster placement has broken down. We will refer to the 15-year-old as Roman for the case study. I was tasked with facilitating the move from Roman's current placement to Paulette's for an initial period of 15 days.

As a part of the Fostering Assessment and Support Team A, my role within the team and towards Paulette was as her supervising social worker. This means that I provided logistical support to her in terms of any new placement, discuss with her the profile of any potential young person to be placed in her care, assist her in making an informed decision whether or not to accept the young person into her home, organise and facilitate the moving of a young person to her care and also making announced and unannounced visits to her home to check on her welfare, wellbeing and care that she is providing to the young person in her care. These planned and unplanned visits are called supervisory visits and are done every four to six weeks. Yearly or tri-annually, I must be present with and support her during her annual reviews with an Independent Reviewing Officer or before the Fostering Panel. I am also available to Paulette through telephone calls or emails in the event there is something to discuss which requires my immediate attention.

In discussing the journey from being advised of the need for the move, to preparing for the move, facilitating the move, debriefing about the move and the outcomes of the move in the days and weeks after, I will be using some key concepts of Bertalanffy's Systems Theory which have been adopted and adapted by others such as Talcott Parsons in the 1950s era and also by one Niklas Luhmann during the era of the 1970s. The purpose of using this theory is to show how the inner workings and processes of the Fostering Team working in tandem with other internal teams, have an influence on Paulette and how she adapts to the significant changes in her daily routine and life because of Roman being placed in her care. Other theories which will also be referenced are Bowlby's Attachment Theory which will show how Foster Carers and Looked after Children form bonds and attachments with each other and how these attachments can be broken or nurtured. In Paulette's case, the similarities and differences between the attachment of her long-term placed child and the respite-placed child will be briefly examined. Additionally, Roman's breakdown in attachment to his previous Foster Carer and his new attachment to Paulette will also be looked at briefly. At a glance, Paulette's demeanour of always having a positive outlook on her role and care given as a Foster Carer will be highlighted about Freud's Positive Psychology Theory and also Carl Roger's Person-Centred Approach.

So, let's start from the beginning. The referral was done internally and came to my attention from the Commissioning and Resources Team (CRT) which is the team tasked with sourcing and building relationships with external placement providers within the United Kingdom. However, the CRT always liaises with internal social workers on the Fostering team in the event there is a carer who is available to accept a young person requiring a placement. Before the referral would have come to my attention, it would have already been through several systems and processes initiated by the social worker allocated to Roman in collaboration with the social worker allocated to Roman's foster carer. A meeting would have already taken place where the request for the move would have either come directly from Roman or his foster carer and the reasons given. Attempts would have been made at this point to see if any interventions could have been done and put in place to prevent the move and repair the relationship between Roman and his foster carer.

When that failed, a profile on Roman would have been drafted, perused, and approved, and then sent to the CRT with a request for a respite placement to be sourced. The request for placement would also state whether the respite placement is to be local or all locations considered. CRT would then have looked at the profile, log into their system as active and then forward Roman's profile with the request for placement to the Fostering and Assessment Team's duty worker. The duty worker then has two options available – either check the foster carers' list and see where there was a vacancy or send Roman's profile and request for placement to every foster carer on the team to see who knew of a foster carer who would be a match for Roman to be placed with. That was how the referral came to my attention and this was evidence of how the various departments worked independently of and in tandem with each other towards the same goal. This is a prime example and explanation of Bertalanffy's Systems Theory and its key concepts of Reciprocal Transactions and Mesosystem which argues that the workings of and relationships between each part of the system directly and sometimes indirectly influences each other (Greene, 2017). The processes that happed before now have influenced me to contact Paulette since I am part of the microsystem and closest to her.

However, before placing a call to Paulette, I printed Roman's profile and had a thorough read of it to not only familiarise myself with the details but also to make a pre-conclusion as to whether Paulette was a good match for Roman to be placed with her. I weigh up the pros and cons holistically and concluded that Roman could be placed with Paulette for the duration of the respite period. However, this was only my initial assessment and I still had to call Paulette and let her make her assessment of the situation after she had considered the pros, cons, and overall risks. Parker (2017) states that assessments in social work should always consider risks to everyone concerned and ways to minimise any risks identified. Further, Milner et al (2015) argue that assessments when placing a child with a foster carer should consider issues and concerns of equality and diversity and whether the needs and best interest of the child will be met by the foster carer.

My assessment found that Paulette had a successful history of fostering young people who were quite like Roman and that seemed to be her area of expertise as a foster carer. Roman was an unaccompanied minor from Afghanistan who had applied for asylum in the United Kingdom and had been placed in the care of the Local Authority since his arrival approximately five years prior. Since then, he has been with two foster carers including the one where the relationship had broken down and where respite was needed from. All of Paulette's past fostering experience had been with unaccompanied minors from either Afghanistan or Iran. This indicated to me that Paulette had a sound understanding of Roman culture, ethnicity, religion, and dietary needs. A cross-check on Paulette's file confirmed this where it stated that she had changed her diet to only include halal foods and had also purchased prayer mats for the young people who had been in her care. She has also attended multiple training sessions on equality and diversity with a specific focus on Muslim identity.

After having satisfied me that Roman was a good match to be placed with Paulette, I called Paulette to discuss with her. I read Roman's profile and went over the key points and areas in the profile which I thought were important. This included Roman's singular interaction with the police where he was cautioned for being in the company of someone carrying a knife and the reasons why his relationship with his current placement had broken down which surrounded the foster carer's lack of understanding of Roman's cultural and religious identity and her lack of providing for his dietary requirements. I explained to Paulette that with her previous and current experience of fostering young men like Roman that I would recommend that she accept the placement for the respite period of 15 days. I impressed her that that was only my recommendation and that I would be further guided by her assessment and decision. My interaction with Paulette was a combination of using the Strengths-Based and Person-Centred Approaches. I highlighted where she showed the most success while placing her at the centre of my assessment and recommendation. I gave her the information and allowed her to use that information, along with what my views and observations were in reaching her conclusions on accepting or rejecting the proposed respite placement.

Fortunately, Paulette decided to accept the proposed respite placement on the condition that it does not extend beyond a maximum of four weeks. She explained that this was because the current young man placed with her had recently begun to act up since he was granted limited leave to remain in the United Kingdom. Paulette stated that she would not want the behaviour of the young man to have any negative influence on Roman and as such she can only provide a four-week respite placement. I agreed with Paulette and further suggested that when Roman begins his placement with her that the three of us would sit down and go over the conditions of the placement. I suggested his curfew time be brought forward an hour from 9 p.m. on weekdays and extended by thirty minutes to 9:30 p.m. on weekends. Paulette agreed with my suggestions and interventions and it was decided that the move would proceed the next day. I relayed the information back to the duty worker and the CRT who planned for transportation for me to collect Roman from his current placement and take him to Paulette's. I also placed a call to his current foster carer to advise her of the move and to Roman to let him know as one of the complaints he made was that his current foster carer was not relaying messages to him promptly. The move went ahead as planned and Roman settled very quickly into living with Paulette and having a

Foster Carer who not only understood his culture and religion but also made provisions for his dietary needs.

In deciding to ask Paulette to offer respite care to Roman, I was ethical in my approach where I made sure that she had all the information about Roman that was known to me and by extension known to Brent Fostering. This transparency of ethics and values was quite important to me in these instances as Perlan (1975) quoted in Gambrill (2017) argues that there is little value in social work where it can't be translated into practice. Further, in disclosing the profile information on Roman to Paulette, I applied both the teleological and the deontological models (Reamer, 1955 in Gambrill, 2017) in handling this ethical dilemma. Firstly, I was quite determined to be as open and honest as possible with Paulette about Roman all within the boundaries of confidentiality between myself as the Supervising social worker and Paulette as the foster carer. Secondly, I weighed up the options of whether or not to disclose information to Paulette and in the end resolved to let her know so that she could decide for herself in her best interest and welfare and also the best interest of Roman. My actions and thought process which influenced my decision making also included applying the person-centred approach to the situation.

Cark Rogers' Person-Centred Approach (Turner, 2017) when applied to social work is where the service user or client is at the centre of any advocacy, interventions, decisions, and ethical considerations undertaken by their allocated social worker and any other professional involved in their lives. In this case, this is exactly what I did before making contact and when it came to making the decision to contact Paulette and asking her to offer respite placement accommodations to

Roman. I considered whether Paulette had the space and time to take on another young person within her home based on the issues and concerns she previously raised with the current young person in her care. Having considered that aspect, I also looked at Paulette was equipped to handle any challenging behaviour Roman may display based on his profile which recorded him as previously having difficulties managing his anger. Keeping Paulette at the centre of my thought process and decision making, I looked at the reasons why the relationship between Roman and his previous foster carer broke down and evaluated whether that same issue may surface during his time placed with Paulette. Going further, I also placed Roman at the centre of me deciding if he should be placed with Paulette by gaining his views on being removed from his current foster placement and being moved to a temporary placement until a more permanent placement can be sourced for him. After ascertaining that it was his wish to be moved, I knew what my next step would be. I satisfied myself that the risks associated with moving Roman to Paulette's for a short period were minimal or non-existent and thus I was confident in my final decision to contact Paulette to discuss her providing respite placement accommodations to Roman.

Chapter Six – Case Study Part Two

During the time that Roman was placed with Paulette, my visits to the home and my observation of the interaction between Paulette and Roman spoke to that of a secure attachment from Roman to Paulette. Secure attachment as conventionalised by Bowlby speaks of a bond created between two persons, usually starting from infancy, which guides interaction, feelings, and personalities (Fonagy, 2018). This secure attachment derived from the fact that Paulette was aware of what Roman needed to make his placement with her work and she did everything that she could to support him and meet his needs. This included having a conversation with him about his eating habits and dietary requirements and her going out and buying the foods and ingredients that he needed. Further, she was quite understanding about the need for her to be flexible in terms of Roman's curfew times as it related to him attending afterschool activities and football practice. I observed with Roman that due to Paulette meeting his needs which were not recognised and met by his former foster carer, Roman developed a secured attachment to her and the relationship between both of them flourished. So much so that as the date for Roman approached for him to leave Paulette and go to his new permanent foster placement, Roman became quite sad about it and asked that he be allowed to remain with Paulette whom he had started to refer to with affection as 'mum'. If I was to go further and apply Bowlby's psychoanalysis approach to secure attachment, Roman's attachment to Paulette could be seen to have followed a primary and a secondary drive. According to Fonagy (2018), Bowlby argued that the primary drive was where Paulette orally and physically recognised and responded to Roman's needs thus causing him to have the secondary drive of forming a bond and an attachment to Paulette.

It was quite interesting to see the attachment theory so prevalent in a fifteen-year-old young person towards his foster carer as my previous studies and knowledge from university predominantly focused on attachment in regards to babies, infants, and adolescents towards their parents or primary caregiver. While that is a natural phenomenon and occurrence, in the case of Roman and Paulette and according to Bowlby in research done by Shemmings & Shemmings (2011), the secure attachment that Roman felt to Paulette might have developed after a period of disorganised attachment to his previous foster carer and within his previous home environment. From Roman's account of his experiences, his previous foster carer did not communicate with him, refused to cater to his dietary and religious needs and more often than not left him to his own devices and to fend on his own. There was no element of care, love or warmth from his previous foster carer so when he received it right from the onset from Paulette, he viewed her as a positive and caring influence and thus developed a secure attachment and bond with her.

In further reflecting on this case study and my advocacy and interventions with both Paulette and Roman, I realised that the balance of power dynamics between social workers and service users is quite delicate and can be both positive and negative. According to Raven & French's Social Power Theory, as argued by Simpson et al (2015), I possessed the information and knowledge about Roman which when disclosed to Paulette influenced her to make a decision and my assessment of that information and knowledge might have played a part in influencing her to make the decision that she made. What would be interesting to find out is if I had held back certain bits of information from her rather than being quite open and transparent with the information held about Roman, would Paulette have reached the same conclusion and decision in allowing Roman to be placed with her for the respite period? Further, what would have been the consequences and impact on the professional relationship between Paulette and me if I had withheld vital information from her and there was an incident or displaying of anger from Roman towards her?

These and other questions were discussed and evaluated during a case review and supervision meeting that I had with my team manager a week after the respite placement ended and Roman went to his new permanent placement. Case reviews and supervision in social work are quite important as they allow for best practises and intervention methods to be revised, discussed, evaluated and assessed to see if they worked, are fit for purpose or need to be changed, amended or adapted (Kadushin & Harkness, 2014). Not only that but it gives a chance for the social worker and manager to determine the best interest of the service user was served. In this case with Paulette and Roman, my team manager helped me to understand and confirm that my actions were fully justified and in line with Brent's policies, procedures, and best practices. She also suggested that I use the experience and knowledge gained as part of my work placement portfolio and also my continued professional development. There was an area for improvement according to my team manager as she suggested that in the future I should consider organising and facilitating an introduction meeting between the foster carer and the young person as an icebreaker before the placement officially begins. This suggestion was noted and would be used in my future practice as a qualified social worker.

Overall, this case study forced me to recognise my role and responsibilities within a much larger system that works in tandem and is inter-dependent of each other in the best interest of the service users we deal with and therefore the decisions and interactions I make can have a negative or positive impact and implications on not only the servicer user but also the system as a whole. In addition, the past and current experiences of service users should be considered when building relationships or deciding on any advocacy or interventions as the outcomes of such can determine and influence what happens to the wellbeing and welfare of said service users. Paulette and Roman's journey through the various strands of a system designed to work in both their best interests was as complex as it was easy. Complex in the sense where Roman had a disorganised placement that did not cater to his needs and where he was longing for that feeling and sense of belonging and care which never materialised and thus so it was easy then to place him in an environment with Paulette where his needs would be met and he would have that secure attachment and strong bond with someone designated to care for him. In conclusion, I have learnt that even though I may not be aware of all the previous decisions and interventions made on behalf of a service user, I have to be mindful that any interventions or decisions I make on their behalf can have lasting positive or negative consequences.

References

Eileen Gambrill, 2017. social work Ethics: The International Library of Essays in Public and Professional Ethics. Routledge, London.

Eraut, M., 2002. *Developing professional knowledge and competence*. Routledge.

Fonagy, P., 2018. Attachment Theory and Psychoanalysis. Routledge, London.

Greene, R.R., 2017. General systems theory. In *Human behavior theory and social work practice* (pp. 215-249). Routledge.

Kadushin, A., Harkness, D., 2014. Supervision in Social Work. Columbia University Press, USA.

Milner, J., Myers, S. and O'Byrne, P., 2015. *Assessment in social work*. Macmillan International Higher Education.

Parker, J., 2017. social work *practice: Assessment, planning, intervention and review*. Learning Matters.

Shemmings, D., Shemmings, Y., 2011. Understanding Disorganised Attachment. Jessica Kingsley Publishers, London.

Simpson, J.A., Farrell, A.K., Oriña, M.M. and Rothman, A.J., 2015. Power and social influence in relationships. *APA handbook of personality and social psychology*, *3*, pp.393-420.

Thyer, B. ed., 2010. *The handbook of social work research methods*. Sage.

Turner, F.J., 2017. social work Treatment. Oxford University Press, London.

Chapter Seven – Asye

On the second day of my ASYE, I was called into the Deputy Manager's office and allocated a case that was already in court and required a Section 7 report to be completed within three short weeks. Now, I had never heard of such a report before and I did not have any prior experience writing court reports. I was not even shown an example of one when I was at university. And now here I was, on my second day as a Newly Qualified Social Worker (NQSW), tasked with competing a Section 7 report. Imagine the pressure and stress I felt at that very moment.

The first thing I did was go straight to the Children Act 1989 and jumped straight to Section 7 to read it in detail and make notes. To be quite honest, it was a bit confusing for me, but I was determined to make both heads and tails of what was required and expected of me in undertaking this Section 7 report.

During my first placement in the Localities Team, I had the opportunity and privilege of befriending and working alongside an excellent and knowledgeable young male social worker who, having only qualified a few years previously, was already a senior social worker and well on his way into Middle Management. So naturally, I turned to him for some advice and guidance on how to go about writing the court report.

Luckily, he had done a few of them before and he not only sat me down and went through all the sections with me and told me what to put on each section, he also sent me two of the most recent ones that he had done so that I could refer to for guidance. He, I must say, had the most positive impact on me during my formative years as a social worker and I still contact him from time to time for advice.

In addition to meeting with this family for who the section 7 report was commissioned, I was also allocated to other families so I had to learn fast to prioritise my work and manage my caseload effectively. On top of that, I still had my ASYE Portfolio and related assignments to complete. This included attending reflective sessions, being observed on visits or at meetings, writing reflective essays, and completing what seemed to be never-ending forms.

In all of this, I had who I considered was the very best team manager and ASYE Supervisor ever. She pushed me to be a better version of myself than I thought I already was. She also pushed me to challenge tick boxes and to be bold on merging my previous experience and knowledge as a Criminology and Youth Work graduate with what I learnt, will learn and come to know as a social worker. I applied that advice and, in my opinion, it made me a better social worker.

During my ASYE, the cases I managed were varied with different complexities to deal with. For context, let me give you a flavour of the cases that I got allocated to me:

1. Parents fighting over who the child should live with. The child is below 10 years of age with English as a

second language, a speech impediment, no boundaries with either parent and previously witnessed DV between parents.

2. Black male teenager with undiagnosed mental health concerns. He was a victim of a stabbing and suffered anxiety and PTSD as a result. He was a very good student and had top grades at college. His fear of being stabbed again caused him to have a minor breakdown where he took a knife and went out in the streets looking for someone to hurt.

3. Black male teenager who was experiencing a breakdown within his adopted family. Parents were quite negative towards him and wanted him to leave their home. He signed himself into Foster Care and began to flourish and gain confidence.

4. Mother of an unborn baby who was attacked by her partner who had multiple personality disorder and mild schizophrenia.

5. A white mid-teen male involved in crime and drugs. He was at risk of CSE and being used for county lines drug running. He was also verbally and physically abusive to his mother who herself smoked cannabis. Family at risk of gang reprisals.

6. Mixed race male in late teens with a high dependency on home-made drugs. He smoked cannabis, was involved with gangs and owed a huge debt to them. His mother excused and protected his behaviour and was an enabler to him. Threats made to them by known and unknown persons.

I could go on and on but I think you get the idea.

Doing the Section 7 court report was a steep learning curve for me as I had to quickly familiarise myself with all aspects of Private Law proceedings. I also had to liaise with our Legal Department, field calls, and emails from child advocates and explain over and over to the legal representatives of the parents that all of their queries had to be addressed to our Legal department. I kept wondering what about that they didn't understand or get as they still kept calling me and sending me emails without copying in our solicitors.

After the report was finished, quality checked and approved by Legal, it was submitted to the court and all relevant parties for perusal. Some of the contents were objected to by the parents but I had all the evidence to support my assessments and decisions and in the end the report was accepted in full by all parties. The case dragged on for months and I had to complete an addendum Section 7 report as the court asked for further information.

I also attended court on two occasions to give evidence, and while I was nervous as heck, one of the magistrates complimented me and stated that the reports were thorough and well-presented and that I defended my recommendations confidently. I was totally pleased to hear that. In the end, the case was transferred to another local authority as the custodial parent moved. I often wondered what was the final outcome of those proceedings.

Not too long after I had completed the Section 7 court report, my team manager called me into her office and told me that she had another court case for me to manage and that it required a Section 37 report to be done at short notice. She explained that the case was currently sitting with another team but no one in that team could do it or even wanted to do it. Further, as she explained to me, I was the only person within our team that had previous court experience. I was shocked by that as there were quite a few Senior Social Workers within the team.

So here I was with my second court case and this time with a Section 37 report to write in less than three short weeks. I knew that was not going to be sufficient time for me to meet with all the family members, get input from other professionals working with the family, meet with the children's respective schools and write a thorough report so I asked my team manager to request an extension from the court through our Legal team. The extension was granted and I got to work.

With this court report, there were lots of allegations and counter-allegations made against the parties from each other so it was quite challenging and sometimes frustrating for me. On top of that, the adults in this case seem be using the children against each other and, apparently forgetting that the proceedings and outcome of the court case would have a real impact on the children involved.

I was mindful of this and at a meeting with the parents, involved family members and the school, I raised this concern and advised the parents that any attempts to manipulate the situation by using the children will be included in my report. This seemed to have an impact as there were no further obvious attempts at manipulation from either side. However, there were signs that the children were being asked to change their accounts of events or were being coached in their responses and this was noted in my final report.

After the final report was submitted to the court and the relevant parties, one side was not happy with the recommendations I made and asked for a second assessment to be undertaken by another social worker, and the Section 37 report to be withdrawn and re-written. Their request was rejected by the court and my report was accepted. However, this did not satisfy that side and they challenged a few of my observations and recordings of conversations and the court asked for an addendum to the report.

The addendum was completed, citing that I stood by the contents of the report, and submitted to the court with further supporting evidence. The court accepted my addendum and supporting evidence. This angered the side and they requested that I be removed as the social worker. However, as there were no safeguarding issues within the family, and as they only became known to us due to the court asking for the Section 37 report to be done, the case was closed to us and the court became the lead agency.

Memorable Moment #2

I was attending court to give evidence on the Section 7 court report that I had completed and submitted. As an ASYE, I could not attend on my own so was accompanied by a senior social worker from my team. She had never undertaken a Section 7 report before and also, had never had to attend court to give evidence. So, this was a first for both of us.

During the proceedings, I gave evidence and answered questions posed to me by the panel of magistrates and from the solicitors representing both the claimant and the respondent. I didn't even realise that I had not referred to my notes when answering the questions until the Senior social worker pointed it out to me during a short recess. She said that she was impressed by the way I handled myself and how confident I was. Further, she stated that she did not think she would have been as composed as I was.

I was thankful for her observations and comments and she provided written feedback for my ASYE portfolio and to my Team Manager. When we got back to the office the next day, she told the entire office about my performance in court and I was congratulated. It was a huge boost to my confidence as a social worker, especially since all the senior social workers in the team at that time, had never done a Section 7 report and had never been to court to give evidence.

Approximately a month later, the court asked for an addendum to the Section 7 report as one of the parties submitted new evidence. That meant that I would have to attend court again. This time, a senior social worker from another team came with me. He was the person I mentioned who gave me a master class on writing court reports. I was more nervous this time around as he would be doing a direct observation on me for my ASYE portfolio.

At the end of the court proceedings, we had a debrief and he was full of praise for me. He said that I had handled all the objections the parties had to Section 7 very well. He also pointed out that the panel of magistrates had made it clear to the objecting parties that the Section 7 report was, in their professional judgement, very thorough and supported by irrefutable evidence. He also said that I should, after my ASYE, consider specialising in writing court reports as part of my continued development.

Both of my appearances at court and the feedback received from the senior social workers and my colleagues, stand out as one of my memorable moments. As it was my first time tackling a Section 7 report, and attending court, I would also count as a pinnacle moment in my social work journey.

Chapter Eight – Challenging Racism and Discrimination

The rest of my ASYE went relatively well with a few challenges and noteworthy experiences in between. One such experience happened when a colleague and I went to a training session that was being organised by the West London Alliance. This training was on Child Protection and Court Skills. Even though I had already completed two court reports by then, I was eager to know more about the court processes and procedures as they related to Social Work.

On the day of the training, my colleague and I met at the office and then headed out to the training location. It was not far from where we were based so we decided to take the bus rather than drive there in her vehicle. Unfortunately, that was a mistake as after we boarded the bus, we realised that there were roadworks and temporary lights in place. We knew then that we were going to be late.

Once we got off the bus, we just had enough time to grab some coffee and a bite to eat and head to the training room. Ahead of us were two other persons seemingly headed in the same direction so we felt a little better knowing that we were not the only ones that were late. The two other persons disappeared around a corner and when we got there, we realise the door leading to the training was right there.

Upon opening the door and stepping in, the facilitator looked up from where she sat and shouted at us not to come in. My colleague and I stood frozen wondering what was happening. The facilitator then asked us to wait outside and she would come and have a chat with us. The other two persons who entered before us were settling into their seats and looked at us with a confused look on their faces.

My colleague and I stepped back outside and waited at the door for a while. When we realised the facilitator was taking a long time to come out, we decided to go across to the kitchenette area to have a seat and wait for her. It was another ten minutes or so before she came out to speak to us. By then we were already halfway through drinking our coffee and eating the breakfast item we had brought.

The facilitator came into the kitchenette and without evening a greeting, she told us that we were late and that we would not be able to enter the training. My colleague and I looked at each other with incredulous looks on our faces. We could not believe what we were hearing. I then turned to the facilitator and told her we were seconds behind the other two who had entered and she dismissed me and said that's not the point.

I asked her what the point was as I'd missed it. She continued to say that we were late and went on about us having coffee and a treat. Mind you, the same two persons before us both had coffee cups with them as well. My colleague was trying to explain about the roadworks and temporary lights but this facilitator was not having it.

While they were both talking, it then got me and I got really upset fast. The other two persons who were allowed to enter the training, even though they were late as well, were not black. My colleague was Latin and I was black. This, I realise, was not about us being late. It was about us being late and something other than white.

I hastily interrupted the now heated conversation between my colleague and the facilitator and asked her point-blank if it was because the other two were white and we weren't that's why they were allowed in. Silence. She didn't answer. But the look on her face gave it all away. I was correct.

Suffice it to say I was now angry. I called her out on her racist attitude and behaviour and my voice started to get loud. My colleague had to touch my arm and tell me to calm down. I was livid. How could this training facilitator, employed to train social workers, practice blatant discrimination?

When she realised that we had sussed her out, she tried to retract her strong objections to us attending the training and said that we can now attend the training but we had to wait until after the first break. I looked at her like are you for real? Do you want us to sit here after you've discriminated against us, and wait until after the first break to go back into the training? When we could just apologise and follow you back into the room? Don't you see anything wrong with that?

By this time, I'd had it and I told my colleague that if she wants to go into the training, she could but I was going back to the office. I told the facilitator that I would be lodging a complaint and that is when she tried to apologise. I told her it was too late to try and apologise and I left. My colleague left with me and we went back to the office where we updated our Team Managers and sent off an email to the training organiser. We have yet to receive an acknowledgment or a response.

Now some of you may say that I overreacted and should have accepted her apology and attend the training. Some of you may even say that I should have used that experience and challenge her with it while in the training. Some of you may even say that I should expect it as it's the norm. Well, it's not the norm for me and will never be the norm for me. And I will never accept being discriminated against either.

And that is one of the problems with some black social workers that I have spoken to over the years. They have normalised being discriminated against treated differently because of their race and ethnicity. They are afraid to challenge and call out racism. Thus, just accept it, deal with it internally and move on. But how can we ever call for change and see that change take place if we don't speak out? How do we expect to be treated equally and respected if we don't fight against the odds?

Well, if you don't want to fight against racism, I will fight against racism and continue fighting against racism wherever I see it within the profession and elsewhere.

Chapter Nine – Critical Reflection

As part of my ASYE process, I had to submit three reflective pieces either on a case that I was managing or something within the profession that had an impact on me. There was on critical reflection piece that I did that the ASYE coordinator of the local authority came to see me personally to have a chat about.

She said that it's rare to see a newly-qualified social worker raise these concerns and that she found my piece refreshing to read. She said that she would share it with managers and asked for my consent to do so. I gave consent but whether she shared it or not I don't know as I never heard anything back.

The piece that I wrote was on how some social workers HEAR to RESPOND, rather than LISTEN to UNDERSTAND. I'll let you read it for yourself.

"In some circumstances and situations, we must and need to LISTEN to UNDERSTAND, rather than HEAR to RESPOND."

I have realised that there are some professionals, social workers included, that have lost the ability to listen effectively, digest and analyse the information presented logically, discuss the options available holistically and compassionately, and then make the necessary referrals and interventions appropriately. The empathy and genuine concern for the welfare of the individual and family seem to have disappeared all in an effort to tick a few boxes and place on record that some form of intervention or service has been suggested and offered. Often enough, while the services and interventions utilised appear to be the ideal ones on paper, these interventions sometimes do more harm than good.

Within Social Services, this haste to refer service users to services and interventions can impact the credibility of the social workers and impact the trust and relationship that social workers build with service users. Service users may think that Brent is all about attempting to treat the problem or issue without first knowing and understanding what the problem or issue is. Further, families may be referred to services that cause them more anxiety and make their initial problem worse. Then the social worker has to go in and not only deal with the initial problem but also the additional concerns that have been caused as a result of the services and interventions they made in the first place. In my practice, I always try to overcome this dilemma by going in, meet with the family, try to understand what the issues and root causes of the issues are, discuss ways in which they can help me to help them, and then suggest any services or interventions which can directly address the issues that they are facing. By doing this, it has been my experience that families are more willing to engage as they feel as if they have been part of the decision-making process as opposed to being told what to do. I simply just listen.

In my studies at university, my colleagues and I were advised that in all aspects of our practice, there would always be a need to have some personal and professional self-reflection. In the case of listening, did we actively listen? Did we fully understand? Did we confirm that what was told to us was understood in the way it was meant to be received? Finally, did we use our understanding to inform our decisions on the next steps? If we did all this, then I assess that we have listened to understand and not heard to respond. However, if we then immediately make decisions on what services the individual or family should receive then we have heard to respond and not listened to understand.

In my practice, I have seen how professionals hear to respond without even meeting the individual or family. They suggest and put in place interventions and services based on what is written in case of notes, summary reports, and referrals. They make contact with the individual or family via telephone or email after referrals have been made. There is no discussion with the family to understand past and present situations, there is no input from the family on what assistance they need, and there is no empathy shown for the difficult and sometimes unavoidable circumstances the individual or family finds themselves. Quite often, there is a culture of victim-blaming where professionals have assumed that the situation the individual or family finds themself in is one of their own makings. This needs to stop and we should practice listening to understand rather than hearing to respond.

In listening to understand, I ask simple questions and allow the service user to speak freely and openly without any interruptions. Even when they go off topic and speak about something else, I let them do so as often during those times you get a sense of where the service is at, what is going through their minds, how they see things, and how they would respond to different services and interventions. I have found that when they start talking about other things, they are indirectly still talking about their issues and problems but in a manner that suits them and their moods. I just listen and take in as much as I can then reflect on it later and find the message in what they were saying. The way that Social Services approaches Child and Family Assessments, allows me to take this approach with the service users. My intervention methods and ways of dealing with service users and other professionals are discussed in supervision with my team manager before they are implemented. This allows collective responsibility to happen, for any perceived risks to be identified, and mitigated.

I was assigned a case of a young person who self-referred himself to services citing that he felt like hurting someone and owned a knife. When the information came in, immediately other professionals jointly working on the case suggested CAMHS involvement, gangs worker involvement, and AST involvement. All this was based on them just receiving and reading the referral. The young person was seen by CAMHS and became agitated and uncooperative because his mental health was being questioned, he was assigned a gangs worker and did not engage because he had no history of being involved with gang activities and AST refused to get involved because he was not at risk of being taken into care.

When I met with the young person, I had already read the case notes and the various interventions and services that had been put in place that yielded no success. The young person was quite apprehensive about meeting me and this showed in his body language and facial expression. He engaged very little in our first meeting so I kept it short. On the second meeting, I started by asking him what he liked to do in his spare time and what he hoped to build a career in. His passion was music and he wanted to be a producer. However, he explained that his passion for music had diminished a little and when I asked why he said that he had been a victim of knife crime eight months prior and since then he has internalised his feelings. He said that when he tried talking to others, he was not listened to, and all everyone wanted to do was label him as both a victim and a perpetrator and he said that he does not want to be known as either.

I asked him how he felt when he was viewed as a victim and as a perpetrator. I asked him how previous professionals approached him and how he felt about their approach. I reminded him about our first meeting and what I had observed about his body language and facial expressions and he confirmed my initial assessment and impression of him and stated that I was the only person to challenge him on his reluctance to engage rather than taking his refusal as him not wanting to engage. I allowed him to lead the initial sessions until we had built up a good rapport and I could see that he had started to trust me. Most times, I just listened to understand his side of things.

Our sessions continued in that fashion where I let him talk about how being stabbed made him feel, what emotions he went through and still goes through. I listened to him talk about his relationship with his family, his friends, his attitude towards education, and how his love and passion for music *were slowly dying. I listened and I understood exactly where he was coming from and what needed to be done. I assessed him and discussed my assessment with him and he not only agreed with my assessment of him but he asked me why the other professionals did not approach him the way I did. I reflected on that question and wondered to myself if that was because I was still relatively new to the profession and was passionate about making a positive difference in the lives of those I work with and on behalf of. Or maybe I placed myself in his shoes and thought about what I would want professionals to do to help me.*

Because I listened to understand, I realise that the best way to help him was to get into the recording studio to work on music. Because I listened to understand, I challenged him to direct all of his raw emotions into producing music. Because I listened to understand, he is now more positive about his future and his career aspirations. Because I listened to understand, I prevented him from being just a statistic with other services and interventions. Because I listened to understand, I was able to help him in the way he needed to be helped.

Spoken Word #1 – Everything Remains the Same

You poured your heart out to others but nothing changes and everything remains the same

You speak of your fears and disclose your insecurities, but nothing changes and everything remains the same

You lay your soul bare and show your absolute vulnerabilities, but nothing changes and everything remains the same

They nod in agreement and feign smiles at the changes you've made, but nothing changes, and everything remains the same

You doubt your abilities and question your capabilities, as nothing changes and everything remains the same

You limit your potential for greatness and suppress your zest for knowledge, as nothing changes and everything remains the same

You confuse your spirituality with the confines of religious doctrines, as nothing changes and everything remains the same

You betray the fight and plight of the ancestors for the easiness of conformity, as nothing changes and everything remains the same

You fall in line with the expectations and classifications of society's justifications, as nothing changes and everything remains the same

You see the best in others even when they show you their worst, but nothing changes and everything remains the same

You play by the rules of the game while others cheat their way to eventually win, but nothing changes, and everything remains the same

Darkness falls, blackness descends, a vast ocean of nothingness appears, you close your eyes and sink into oblivion.

Finally, you open your eyes and see the truth as the truth should be seen.

You open up your understanding, to the knowledge that is there to be gleaned.

You focus your mind on the spirituality of humanity and the morality of society.

You see the reflection in the mirror and you are released from all pain and sorrow.

You look beyond the limitations of the horizons and realise there's hope for tomorrow.

You shake off the stereotypical labels that's were designed to keep you shackled.

You break free from the chains and restraints of your internal strife and battle.

It's now absolutely crystal clear and you are determined to conquer your fear.

For everything changes and nothing remains the same.

Chapter Ten – SWET Court Report

During the last few weeks of my ASYE, I was again given a case that eventually ended up in court and I was asked to do another court report. This time, I had to do a Social Worker's Evidence Template (SWET) report. This term was alien to me and I had to once again go and speak to my mentor and ask him for assistance and guidance. He had a few that he had done previously and he sent them to me so that I could have a look and get an idea of what was required. He even went as far as booking a meeting room so that we could go through the template section by section.

The SWET is a report used by Local Authorities when applying to the court for a legal order for a child or children. This is usually for a Care Order to bring the child or children into the care of the local authority who will share Parental Responsibility for the child or children. Quite often, the child or children are placed with approved Foster Carers or designated and approved extended family members.

Removing a child or children from their parents or guardian is a last resort mechanism that is used to safeguard. This is when it is deemed unsafe for the child or children to remain with their parents or guardians. Before legal proceedings can be imitated, the Local Authority must prove that it has exhausted all other avenues to work with and assist the family in staying together.

The safeguarding concerns in this instance were for a young baby whose mother had severe mental health issues and had been sectioned several times. Further, mother had taken the baby to abandoned buildings, left her soiled and dirty, and had even taken her outside of London. This was while she was on day leave from the hospital.

The complicating factor, in this case, was that the maternal side of the family was being quite obstructive to Social Services and refusing to grant access to the mother and baby. On one hand, they would say to us that they need help and on the other hand they would do their very best to frustrate interventions and strategies. From the onset, I knew it would be a difficult case.

Because we were not being allowed access to the mother and baby, my team manager directed me to request the police for them to undertake a welfare check. When the police got to the house, they were prevented from making peaceful entry by the mother. The officers were concerned about her aggressive and irrational behaviour, and due to her extensive mental health history and recent hospital admissions, they decided to force entry to the flat.

What they found inside was shocking. The flat was in a mess and quite unsuitable for a baby. Therefore, the officers had no choice but to place the baby under Police Protection and into the care of the local authority. The baby was placed with an approved foster carer and the local authority immediately issued proceedings.

We first applied for the court for an Emergency Care Order and this was granted. However, an Emergency Care Order is time-limited up to a maximum of 10 days – which means that I had to move pretty quickly in completing the SWET to apply for an Interim Care Order. I poured through all the previous referrals and case notes, medical and mental health reports, police notifications, and reports and also included assessments from what little interactions I had had with the family.

The first draft of the SWET was terrible and the information was all over the place and not collated. I was stressed out and felt that I was left on my own to do this report. Luckily, a senior social worker who had recently joined the team a few months prior, highlighted that as an ASYE, I should not be doing the SWET on my own. Either she raised it with the managers or I raised it and the SWET was passed over to her to complete. To say that I was relieved was an understatement.

The senior social worker took the first draft of the SWET that I had done and she worked her magic on it. She told me that she would use the same information that I had put into the SWET, organise it sequentially and add her assessments and analysis to it. She also went further back with the chronology than I did. In the end, she produced a world-class SWET (in my opinion) and that was submitted to the court and the Interim Care Order was granted. I told her that I would keep an anonymised and redacted copy of the SWET for future reference.

I often reflect on that my experience and think about how stressed and unsupported I felt before she offered her help. My Team Manager, at that time, was dealing with two other court cases and most probably assumed that since I'd completed court reports before that I would be okay on my own with a SWET. I blame myself for not speaking up and asking for help. I think I was both grateful and overwhelmed by the trust and added responsibilities and didn't want to appear as if I could not cope. I've learnt from that.

Since then, I've been more vocal in asking for help and admitting when I'm not able to cope. I've had to learn that to grow and develop as an effective social worker, it's important to learn from others as well as teach others.

Memorable Moments #3

I celebrated a milestone birthday during my ASYE. It was February 2020, a few weeks before the first lockdown. Usually, the team and other colleagues join together, take up a collection and buy a card and a small present. However, in addition to that, I wanted to do something for them as a way of showing my appreciation for the support they had given since I started my ASYE that past September.

There was a medium size kitchen on the ground floor of the building so I thought that I would prepare lunch for everyone. There were five teams in the building with between 8-11 persons in each team. It was a huge task but I was determined to do it. So, I spoke to the Service Manager, told her if my plans, and she permitted me to proceed.

My brother is a trained chef so I enlisted his services. Together, we came up with a very simple menu that consisted of baked chicken, baked fish, festival rice (rice with raisins, bell peppers, and sweet corn), and macaroni pie. He also did a delicious sauce as well.

On the day of the luncheon, the entire building was wafted with the sweet aromas of my brother's cooking. My team members and other colleagues took turns coming down to the kitchen to watch my brother in his element. I mean, he is a great cook and skilled in his techniques.

When the luncheon was ready to be served, staff members came down to the largest conference room which was next to the kitchen. It was such a sweet moment to see everyone eating together, sharing laughs and just forgetting about any work-related issues and concerns for a couple of hours. I stood at the entrance to the room and just took it all in.

My brother got numerous compliments, as was expected, and some of my colleagues asked him for the recipe for his signature sauce. Sadly, this was a closely guarded secret so he was not able to share it with them. However, he shared his details with them as he also does private catering for small groups and functions.

At the end of the luncheon, some colleagues took away some of the leftovers as I had also provided disposable containers. The rest that was left, the security guard and I packaged it up, took it out into the community, and distributed it to the homeless persons we saw in the area daily. It was indeed a proud and memorable moment and experience for me.

Chapter Eleven – Take It on the Chin Aleski

There was another incident that had a profound impact on me and opened my eyes to the extent others will go to tarnish your reputation and give you a bad name. This incident included one of my colleagues, who was also doing her ASYE and happened on a day when I was assigned to the duty phone. She was of Asian descent and as you know I am a black male. Here is what transpired.

A call came through for her on the duty line from a school that is one of her young people attended. They wanted an update on the case and wanted to provide her with some information as well. I called her into the duty room to take the call and reminded her that if the call was going to be long, to have the school call her back on her direct number or she can give them a call. I said this as it was the rule that we should not take case calls on the duty line as it should for emergency and MASH calls only.

This social worker did not acknowledge or respond to me and proceeded to take the call. After about ten minutes, she was still on the call and it appeared as if it was going to be a long call. She was even sat perched on the desk while on the call. I signalled to her and whispered that she should ask the school if she can give them a call back from her direct line or mobile number. She waved me off quite rudely. There was a senior social worker and another ASYE social worker in the room and they looked at me and shook their heads.

Another ten minutes or so went by and again I signalled to her and reminded her that she was on the duty phone and it needed to be kept free for emergencies and referrals. Again, I whispered. She looked at me, covered the microphone part of the handset, and in a rude manner, dismissed me and said it was a school that she was speaking to. The other two workers in the room looked up at her and one of them said, "But that's the duty phone."

I left the room, as I was quite annoyed at the social worker on the phone. The practice consultant for the team was in her office and I went to have a word with her. I asked her to remind the team that the duty phone was to be kept free for emergencies and referrals and that I everyone should take their calls on their direct line or mobile.

She asked me what had happened and I explained the situation to her. As I was in her office, the social worker must have finished with her call as poker her head in the Practice Consultant's office, saw me there, and then went back to her desk.

I finished my conversation with the Practice Consultation and went back to the duty desk. A few minutes later, the Practice Consultant came out of her office and went to the photocopying machine. The social worker, who was on the duty phone earlier, went up to get and almost on cue, she started to cry real loudly and saying that she wanted to make a complaint on me as I rudely interrupted her call this morning, shouted at her while she was on the phone with the school and that made her embarrassed.

The Practice Consultant took her into her office and closed the door. My two colleagues who were in the duty room earlier had stepped out and went they came back and I told them what had just happened, they could not believe it. They assured me that as they were witnessed what had happened if anything had to come of it, they would tell the Practice Consultant what had truly happened.

I don't know what was said in that room that day, but nothing more was said about the situation and everyone just moved on. Also, the Practice Consultant had left the team and we had a new one. That social worker and I didn't speak at all after that incident and to be honest, I preferred it that way. I don't like to be lied to and I was not going to give her the opportunity to lie to me again.

I steered clear of her and only interacted with her when discussing cases. For me, I didn't have to have a personal relationship with her. I would still be professional towards her and work in the best interests of the children and families we were working with.

A couple of months later, that same social worker and I were on duty together. By then, we were all working from home due to the coronavirus pandemic. As both of us were on duty, we would alternate between the phones and the duty email. One of us would take the duty phone in the morning while the other checks the duty email inbox. Then after much, we would switch. That was how it always worked.

So that morning before 9 a.m., in the team WhatsApp group, I announced that I would take the duty phone in the morning and then take the duty email inbox in the afternoon.

Everyone read the message almost immediately, including that social worker. So, imagine my surprise when a few minutes past 9 a.m, I get an email from that social worker, with the Team Managers copied in, saying that she was going to log onto the duty phone in the morning.

I replied and stated that I had already logged on to the duty phone and had said it in the group chat. The social worker replied and once again lied and boldly stated that she had not read the message and that she does not check the group chat. I was dumbfounded. I went back to the chat, confirmed the time that she had read the message and once she was shown the evidence, she relented.

A few days later, in a team meeting, she brought it up again and tried to play the victim. That created an argument and voices got loud, including mines, as I was not going to allow her to once again lie her way into being seen as a victim. Even other colleagues tried to tell her that she was in the wrong but she didn't want to hear it.

Some colleagues told her that this was not the time and place for her to raise something that had already happened and was settled but still she didn't want to hear it. So, before things got even worse, I announced that I was going to leave the meeting and I signed out.

A couple of weeks after the team meeting, my team manager called me on the phone and told me that the social worker had filed an official complaint against me and she wanted to hear my version of events. She said that the complaint related to the duty room incident, the duty task incident, and the team meeting incident. She also said that the social worker was alleging that I was aggressive towards her, had directed comments towards her in the which made her feel targeted and that I intimidated her.

I said that I was happy to have a three-way meeting with the social worker to sort this out. My team manager agreed to set this up and also include the new Practice Consultant as well since he had chaired the team meeting when things got a. It heated. She, my team manager, stated that's she would be speaking to the other members of staff to get their views and I insisted that this happen.

Before the meeting, I sent my manager all the evidence that I had which included the record of the WhatsApp group chat, emails, and a written statement. In the written statement I detailed the chronology of events which proved that the social worker was making things up and blatantly lying on me to make herself a victim. I also reminded my team manager that there were witnesses to all the events and they were more than happy to provide an account.

During the meeting, each one of us was given the chance to speak on the events. The social worker went first since she was the one who had lodged the complaint. As you can imagine, and even with hard proof that she was lying, she gave an alternative version of events.

When challenged on this, she altered her story and said that complaint was less about what had happened and more about working together as a team abs treating each other with respect. She even went as far as to say that she did not feel safe and supported working with me. When my team manager asked her to explain why she made that statement, she could not even answer.

When it was my turn to speak, I said that the evidence shows that she, the social worker, was lying and manufacturing versions of the events and I did not appreciate that. I said that the use of the words 'aggressive' and 'intimidating' to describe me was problematic at best and had stereotypical racial undertones to them. I ended by saying that as a black male social worker, this could have an impact on my career and this needs to be addressed. However, at that meeting, it was not addressed at all.

When we had both spoken, my team manager and practice consultant both shared their views and thoughts on the situations. They then advised us both to put any personal feelings aside and continue working professionally with each other. I told both of them that although I did not think that the meeting helped or addressed any of the real issues, I was prepared to move forward. I left that meeting feeling powerless. I'll explain why in the next chapter.

Chapter Twelve – Being Stereotyped, Racialised and Silenced

The reason why that meeting left me feeling powerless was less about what had happened in the meeting and more about what had transpired between the incident and the meeting and after the meeting. You see, after the incident, I had several informal and formal meetings regarding the incident with my Team Manager. These meetings occurred as part of my case management supervision, personal supervision, and the meeting to formally and officially respond to the complaint made against me by the social worker.

In the pre-meetings, I protested my innocence, gave accounts of what had actually transpired, and also provided evidence to prove that I was in the right. In these meetings, I spoke about how it felt to be lied to, and how it had and was affecting my mood. In these meetings, I asked and pleaded for the social worker to be held accountable for her blatant lies and attempts to tarnish my reputation.

However, in these meetings, I was told that I could not call the social worker a liar or say that she had lied. In these meetings, I was told that I had to be careful how I worded my response to the complaints and what I was going to say during the official complaints meeting. In these meetings, I was reminded that I was black and the other social worker was of Asian descent. In these meetings, I was advised that if I protested too much, because of my Caribbean accent, I could be stereotyped.

In these meetings, I was told that even though the other social workers' statements said that I was not at fault, the complaining social worker would not be accused of lying. In these meetings, I was told to just take it on the chin, forget about it, chalk it up to experience and move on. In this meeting, I was advised that since I was black, it would be much easier to believe that I was and had been aggressive and intimidating. Even though the evidence proved otherwise. In these meetings, I was rendered powerless to do anything.

After the official complaint meeting, I again had a few informal chats with my team manager. In these meetings, she told me reminded me about how hard it was to be a black social worker, especially a black male social worker. She said that the colour of my skin would be an issue to colleagues and clients alike and that I should learn to accept it and deal with it. She said that few challenges to this are ever successful, while the majority are unsuccessful and spells the end of one's career.

Even after those meetings, I still felt like something was amiss and that that social worker has essentially gotten away with her lies and false accusations. That did not sit well with me and my team manager can tell you I raised it at every single personal supervision that we had. And I got the same response – forget it and move on. It was only a few months later that I found out that that same social worker, in her previous job, had filed a grievance against her managers and the grievance was upheld.

When I spoke to my manager about this and asked if she was aware of this, she said that she was. The look on her face alone told me all that I needed to know. I had been told to forget it and move on as it was feared that this social worker would file another grievance if her case fell through. You see, I was black, my team manager was black, the practice consultant was black and she was of Asian descent. The perfect argument for a complaint/grievance of collusion.

Around that same time, there were heightened tensions around the world involving targeted violence against black people, especially black men. This inspired me to write the spoken word below as I felt hurt, frustrated and angry at how I had been treated and how other young black men were being singled out and treated.

Spoken Word #2 – I Am Black

Excuse me.

May I have your attention?

Can you hear me?

I have got something to mention.

By way of introduction

I am a humble black man with a university education.

I am a father, a husband, a brother, an uncle, a nephew, a son

Simply speaking I'm just a regular person.

But of course, you do not see that?

All you see is the colour of my skin – Yea I am black.

Now has your opinion of me changed?

Am I now something that is strange?

All this just because I am black?

You think I am undereducated, uneducated, gang and drug-related, fabricated and unregulated.

You think I am a product of a broken home, a dysfunctional home, a fatherless home, or an unloving home.

You call me aggressive, repressive, resistive, and even uncooperative.

You call me an animal, a criminal, I am unemotional and I am confrontational.

All this because my skin colour is BLACK.

I am marginalised. I am stigmatised. I am stereotyped. I am sexualised. I am fetishised. I am brutalised. I am racially profiled. I am 'blackmatised'.

I am guilty even though no crime has been committed.

I match the description even if it is an alien.

You stop and search me in a bid to unnerve me.

You frame me so you can imprison me.

You kill me just because you do not like me.

You do not like me just because I am a black king.

I am a black king so you do not like me.

I am black so you 'blackmatise' me.

My blackness seems to be your number one enemy.

Chapter Thirteen – Take It on the Chin, again!

I would have liked to say that that was the only time I was advised to take it on the chin, forget it and move on. Unfortunately, it was not as at the very end of my ASYE, leading into the first months of my Post ASYE year, another incident happened. This time it was while I was writing my second SWET for one of my cases that were in court. And this time, it involved a senior social worker who was seconded to the post of Practice Consultant within our team.

I had just received the good news that I had completed and passed my ASYE and was now a substantive social worker. This was another accomplishment that I could add to my list and be proud of. I no longer had to complete a portfolio to be assessed and I no longer had to use the acronym ASYE in front of my name in my email signature and when completing episodes on Mosaic. You just don't know how good that felt.

It was around the same time that a case I was allocated has been escalated and was being prepared for court. It involved a child under the age of five who presented at the hospital with unexplained injuries including broken bones. The parents had already signed a Section 20 agreement and the Local

Authority was seeking an Interim Care Order and that required me to complete a SWET report for the court.

Now that I was a substantive social worker, I could complete the SWET on my own without having to pass it over to another qualified social worker. And this time, I had less than a week to complete it as the case was listed for an emergency hearing at court. I collated all the information and stayed up all one night and completed the SWET report in one go. For those of you who know what a SWET report is and who have completed one before, you know that it's no easy feat and completing it in one sitting was a challenge in itself.

I submitted the SWET report to my team manager and also the service manager for their perusal and feedback. I was asked to do some minor amendments before it was sent off to the legal team for them to quality assurance before filing with the court and relevant parties. After that, it was just to wait for any submissions from the parents or child advocate in advance of the court hearing.

With the court hearing coming up in a few days, I still had to do hospital visits, discharge meetings and preparing the transfer documents. This was for the case to go to the Looked After Child team once the hearing was over and if the Interim Care Order was granted. Doing all this stressed me out and I was having sleepless nights and unsettled days at work. I just wanted this case to be over with so that I could take a few days off and recuperate.

However, things came to a head when the newly appointed Practice Consultant started micro-managing the team. Everyone was upset about her management style and made it known to the Team Manager. However, rather than address it, we were told to give her chance and try and work with her. Nothing else was done. The unity within the team started to disintegrate and team members started to work from home more often.

The issue that I had with the Practice Consultant was that's she would send me an email and within five minutes she would call to discuss the email. Further, if an email came to me and she was copied in on it, she would proceed to respond okay my behalf and agree to meetings or actions without even checking with me. My anxiety was slowing building up and I was starting to feel demoralised.

There was one day I was fielding calls and emails from her and our legal team for the entire day and I had forgotten to have lunch. So, at 4 p.m. I decided to pack up, go home, have a rest, get something to eat and then continue working. As I was walking to ways the lift, the Practice Consultant called and asked me if I had seen her email. I explained to her that I was not feeling well as I had not eaten all day and would look at the email when I get home.

However, she wanted me to set up my workstation again and look at the email and complete the task before going home. I told her I'm not able to do that as I was not feeling well and needed to go home and have a rest. She completely ignored what I had said and continued to demand that I stayed at the office until the task was compared. By this point I was getting angry and my anxiety level was through the roof.

I got to the lift, got in with another colleague and as soon as the door closed, I slumped against the sides and started to have a panic attack. I could not breathe. I told the Practice Consultant that I was unwell, feeling frustrated and the conversation with her was causing me distress. Again, she ignored what I was saying and continued talking so I told her that I did not want to talk to her and I hanged up the phone. My colleague helped calm me down me took me home in her car.

I got home and went straight to bed without even eating. Later that night I got up, had something to eat and then signed on to look at the email. I kid you not, it was a task from the legal team that was not due until the following week could have been done the following day or before the end of the week. Seeing this upset me even more and because I didn't want her to ask me about it anymore, I compared the task and sent it off. I then sent an email to my team manager asking for a meeting.

The next day while I was out on a visit, several emails came in addressed to me and as usual, the Practice Consultant was answering them even before I could read them. Then she emailed me asking me for an email address. I replied that I was out and that she should look at the previous emails she was copied into for the email address. She replied and said that it would be quicker for me to search for it and send it to her. I reminded her that I was out on a visit and was using my mobile phone so could not search for it.

Lo and behold she called me and still demanded that I stop whatever I was doing and somehow use my phone to search for the email address she wanted. I told her that I was out, could not search for it and did not want to continue the conversation as I could already feel myself becoming frustrated, angry and anxious. I told her that I would be putting the phone down and then I did.

In less than five minutes, here comes an email to me, with the team manager copied into it, telling me that I was being uncooperative and was rude in putting down the phone on her.

I didn't reply to her but replied to my team manager with a second request to have a meeting.

When I eventually spoke to my Team Manager, she empathised with how I was feeling and assured me that she would speak to the Practice Consultant. She said that it was probably the pressures of stepping into a management role that drive the actions of the Practice Consultant and again asked that I give her some more time to find her feet. I had lots of respect for my team manager as I had known her from the very first day of my first placement, so I agreed. In hindsight, I wish I didn't and had insisted on the meeting going forward.

The Practice Consultant not only continued with her micromanaging style but she also started to demand that I change the analysis and recommendations into my assessments to suit her management oversight. For example, if I recommended that a case be closed and no further action is taken, she would ask me to change it and recommend a Child in Need Plan. I would then challenge that order and use the threshold criteria to argue that a Child in Need plan was required.

However, she would ignore my rationale and still assign a Child in Need plan episode to me that had no substantive actions except for referrals to other provisions to me made. Often, these referrals were already part of the closure process. Even some professionals did not understand why a Child in Need plan was implemented if the only actions were referrals. To me, I think it was all a power play and an element of control.

The Practice Consultant would also go on to say to my team manager that I was challenging her decisions too often.

And that at one time I used the phrase 'in my professional judgement' to her and she thought that it was inappropriate for me to say to her as she was a manager.

When my team manager relayed that to me, I was confused. I asked her if I, as social worker, was not supposed to use my professional judgment and I was told yes but the Practice Consultant felt that I used it against her to suggest that my professional judgement trumped her directions on cases.

I explained to my team manager that I feel sometimes that managers forget that the social workers are the ones on the ground meeting with the families and professionals. We are the ones requesting and collating evidence from various sources and analysing the evidence. We are the ones who are having the network meeting and getting feedback from all stakeholders.

So, if the professional network, along with the social worker, concludes that there is no cause for concern and there are no safeguarding concerns following the interventions and strategies put in place during the assessment, why would a manager overlook all that and go against the recommendations of the social worker and the professionals? Especially if the risks in the initial referral have been addressed and managed.

My team manager stated that she understood my views and accepted them. However, I was advised to go with what the Practice Consultant directed, even if I don't agree with it. I told my team manager that I could not agree to that as it was my name that would appear on the assessment and I can't sign off on something that I didn't agree with.

Even when we had a meeting and the Practice Consultant lied in the meeting, and I called her out on it, after the meeting I was told that even though what she said was a lie, I should not have called her a liar. I was supposed to take it on the chin, forget about it and move on. I was not allowed to defend myself and my reputation. I was not supposed to speak up for myself. I was simply expected to take it on the chin, forget it and move on.

Chapter Fourteen – Youth Trust Research

After the incident with the Practice Consultant, my team manager reshuffled the team and I was once again under her direct supervision. The Practice Consultant still evaluated some of my cases, and I still challenged some of her directions on my allocated cases. However, I did not dwell on that or let that distract me from progressing in my career. I was not focused on the next stage of my social work journey and that was to develop a specialism.

As you might remember, my undergraduate degree was in Criminology and Youth Studies. I wanted to merge aspects of that with my social work practice in an official capacity. There were lots of strategies is learn while undertaking the course which I thought would work well within social work. I began to experiment with different concepts and tools that I could bring to social work.

During both my social work placements and my ASYE, I gathered and collated data from the young people that I worked with. I asked them if they were interested in contributing to the research that I was doing and the majority of them agreed. It was explained to them that my research was about the way young people viewed trust among themselves and the people around them. I was interested in finding out if there were variations to the level of trust that young people placed in themselves, their families, their peers, and other people they interacted with – including social workers.

The reason why I decided to research this area was that, over the years of my social work journey, I had seen how young people were wary of social workers. I had seen how they use any excuse, reason, and opportunity not to speak to social workers, be reluctant and selective when forced to speak to them. I had observed their body language and seen the feedback and views they gave on the assessment process how they were portrayed by social workers.

The young people that I had spoken to had this to say about social workers:

1. They try to put words in your mouth and read too much into situations.
2. Social workers act as if they have never done anything wrong when they were my age.
3. Why do they always have to assume the worst, or instantly believe we are being abused?
4. I told my social worker the truth but she kept asking me stupid questions as if she did not believe me.
5. I'm 16 and I get spoken to as if I'm five years old.
6. I think some social workers are prejudiced against black families. Especially if the social worker is white. I don't trust their motives.
7. Some social workers like to create and see division, problems, and conflict within families. It's like that's their main aim.

8. They (social workers) act like they are God and that they have all the answers.
9. I don't like them, plain and simple. I don't trust them at all.
10. I bet you social workers and their families are worse than us they get away with it.

What's interesting is that I've seen and experienced some of the very things the young people have complained about regarding social workers. I've seen some social workers exploit the power they held over families. I've seen some social workers go into the homes of families and bully them into submission. I've seen some social workers threaten families into cooperating and then turn around and accuse them of disguised compliance. I mean I think I have seen it all so nothing surprises me any more within social work.

There were times when I felt ashamed of being a social worker. Especially when I heard families recount past experiences they've had with social workers. I've seen a young person pull out old assessment reports and point out where social workers had been quite disparaging towards them. They painted the young person as 'weird, vague and having a lack of awareness and understanding of what is in their best interest'. This young person disclosed that that made them feel very upset and added to their low confidence and insecurities. And because of that, their grades at school suffered and they became withdrawn.

Early on in my social work journey, I made a commitment to be a different kind of social worker than I'd seen and heard about. And hearing from that particular young person made me reaffirm that to myself. I pledged right then and there to be the kind of social worker that I would have wanted for myself or my family.

Chapter Fifteen – Operation Direct Work

The new me as a social worker decided to focus more on young people's views and feelings and give them priority over what was written in referrals and previous reports. Now, don't get me wrong or misunderstand me. I still read the reports and referrals to get an overview of the work that has been done with the young person, however, I allowed the young person to tell me in their own words how they felt, what their views were and what they needed to be helped with.

You would be surprised to hear how many young people say that they've never had that before. They've never had someone ask about and listen to their voice. Trust me when I say, it makes all the difference in the world to them.

In putting young people first, I also decided to try a new method of undertaking direct work with young people. I wanted to see how allowing them to take the lead in meetings and sessions will impact them and their engagement. It was a trial-and-error situation but I was willing to put the work in. With the blessing and go-ahead from my Team Manager, I embarked on Operation Direct Work.

Operation Direct Work was about finding new and creative ways to interact with young people. Using 'Three

Houses' had been done to death and young people were getting fed up with it. The Signs of Safety approach to direct work was not working, in my opinion, as it was too structured and mechanical. There was no room for a comprehensive and holistic approach.

Using three-set headings in undertaking direct work with young people limited their responses and in so doing, it limits follow-up and greater exploration of issues and concerns raised. For example, asking a young person what's working well for them will most likely elicit a very short and basic answer from them.

Same with asking them what are they worried about and what they would like to happen. Any variations of these three questions would more than likely result in the same thing – limited engagement from young people. That is why I told my team manager that a new and creative way of undertaking direct work with young people needs to happen.

The very first young person I was allocated after I ran my idea by team manager was a young man who presented with suspected mental health issues. He was black, in his first year of college, and an aspiring music producer. You might remember him as I've mentioned him before in Chapter Nine. I wrote a critically reflective piece about my interactions with him.

During my time with him, I found out that he made beats in his spare time and an idea came to me. I asked him if he was willing to try a new way of communicating his feelings and he said he was up for it. Even though he would talk openly in our sessions together, I got the feeling that he was struggling to properly express his feelings about various situations in his life. It just felt as if he was saying the words with no real depth behind them. And I wanted him to go deeper within himself.

I didn't know if it would work but I asked him to think about a particular time in his life that we had spoken about before and to make a beat that represents his feelings and emotions at that time. He agreed and a few days later he sent me the beat. When I listened to it, it was dark, scary, angry, and hurtful.

I arranged to meet him the next day at the office and we listened to the best together. I told him what I was hearing him say within the best and he looked at me with a shocked look on his face. He told me that was exactly how he felt. As we continue to listen to the beat, he closed his eyes and for the first time in all of our sessions, he showed real emotions.

We continued operating that way where we would select a period in his life and he would make a beat to represent how he felt during that time. We would then meet and talk about the beat and his feelings. In a way, this was therapeutic for both of us.

As well as him learning more about himself and how to channel his feelings and emotions, it helped me to also think about ways in which I could channel and manage my feelings, views, and emotions when it came to the challenges and experiences I faced in my job and career.

With this young man, he was eventually discharged from Social Services involvement and agreed to access Talk Therapy when and if he required it. He was also discharged from CAMHS as they concluded that he did not have any mental health issues or concerns. He just hadn't processed situations and experiences in his life that had impacted him in some way.

Before I ended my involvement with him, I put him in touch with an established music producer and a recording artist. The producer invited him into the studio for a masterclass and the recording artist bought one of his beats and recorded a fantastic song. I also took a few of his beats and together we collaborated where I recorded my spoken word pieces to his beats.

I last heard from this young man when I reached out to him to check on how he was doing and asked him to provide some feedback on my interactions with him. He stated that he was doing well and sent in the following feedback:

Aleski is probably one of, if not, the best social workers I have interacted with over the course of my life. He is able to understand and identify with a certain background that youths in today's society feel they can't discuss or talk about with those that work for organisations such as the Social Services.

Throughout my meetings with Aleski, I felt comfortable talking about things that I felt as though I could not discuss with any other social worker. This is what the youth of today's society needs if we want to see progress and change. Social workers I'm used to working with are normally either too intrusive or will 'work' with me but I would still see no particular change.

Aleski took actual interest and was even able to help me sell a couple of instrumentals produced by me. We even joined together and I made some beats which he has performed his spoken word poetry on, touching on issues such as mental health and racism.

He continues to show support even after the closure of my case, helping me with my music as much as possible, ensuring that I'm functioning well. Those who have a chance to work with Aleski are extremely lucky as I do not doubt in my mind that they will receive the help they truly need with him as their social worker.

I showed his feedback to my team manager and she commend me on the difference I had made in this young man's life. And to be quite honest, this was probably one of the best feedbacks I have ever received from a young person thus far.

Spoken Word #3 – Mental Health

The voices in my head are loud, aggressive, demanding, frustrating, confusing, and never-ending.
They tell me I am worthless.
They tell me I am helpless.
They tell me to hurt someone.
They tell me do not to trust anyone.
They fill me with fear and dread.
They tell me I will be better off dead.
I try to fight them, to reason with them, to silence them, to banish them, to let my positive thoughts be louder than them.

SHUT UP. BE QUIET. LEAVE ME ALONE. STOP TALKING TO ME.

But no matter how much I try and I try and I try. I feel defeated, exhausted, overwhelmed, alone and all I do is cry.
I long for and crave those rare moments of peace, of silence, of clarity, where I can function with some sense of normality.
On the outside, I laugh but I am hurting inside.
On the outside, I am calm but there is a storm inside.
On the outside, there's hope but there is despair inside.

On the outside, there is sunshine but it is raining inside.

On the outside, success but I feel like a failure inside,

On the outside, I may seem fine while my mental health declines.

I ask for help but I am ignored, I am marginalised, I am stereotyped, I am ostracised, I am victimised, I am stigmatised.

YOU ARE CRAZY. YOU ARE UNSTABLE. YOU ARE UNBALANCED. YOU ARE INSANE.

These names make me feel degraded, unsupported, mistreated, forsaken, suicidal, and in a fight for my survival.

I do not want to be subjected to observation and medication when you do not understand my life and my situation.

See me, so you can

Understand me, so you can

Know me, so you can

Hear me, so you can

Believe in me, so you can

HELP ME.

HELP ME.

HELP ME.

Do not define me by my temporary inability to think rationally and behave appropriately. Do not underestimate my understanding of my role to get my mental health issues under control.

YOU ARE SOMEBODY. YOU ARE WORTH IT. YOU MATTER. YOU BELONG. YOU ARE STRONG.

This is what I want to hear. This is what I need to hear. This is what I hope to hear. Affirm in me that I am more than just an extension of my ALLEGED mental health.

Chapter Sixteen – Paradigms of Youth Trust

The trust that young people developed in me did not do amiss and contribute to the research I was undertaking in the dimensions of trust that young people placed in themselves and others. The research duration was over both my placement and halfway into my ASYE. At the end of the research and after analysing the data collected, I concluded that there are at least six levels of trust among young people.

The data showed that young people's level of trust started with themselves and expanded out towards their interactions. As it extends out, their trust levels, the priority of trust and stability of trust decreases. Those at the furthest end of young people's trust spectrum fall into two categories. The first is absolutely no trust and the second is the flexibility of trust. In the flexibility of trust, persons here have the opportunity to prove their trustworthiness and move to higher levels.

These levels of trust, in order of priority, are as follows:

P1 Themselves – The only area of complete and honest trust even though there may be concerns surrounding coming to terms with any self-identified vulnerabilities.

P2 social media – Total anonymity is key in this level of the trust paradigm. Young people using 'burners' tend to trust other 'burners' especially if they share commonalities.

P3 Family, Friends & Handlers – In this level, trust varies depending on who is seeking that trust and heavily depends on loyalty, confidentiality and fear.

P4 Professionals – Young people have limited trust in professionals due to the mandatory reporting requirements and in this paradigm, trust is earned and not freely given.

P5 Law Enforcement / State Authority – This group is outside of the main circle as there is absolutely no trust in this paradigm as it includes the police and the courts. Trust in this paradigm either means 'snitching' or 'blackmail'.

P6 Others – Trust here is hit and miss and thus the reason it sits outside the main circle. If there is no interaction then trust is irrelevant. Trust only comes into play if there is some interaction. Persons in this paradigm can earn their way into the top levels as time goes by.

I also came up with a visual representation of my findings in addition to a brief explanation of each level. It is entitled "The Paradigms of Youth Trust."

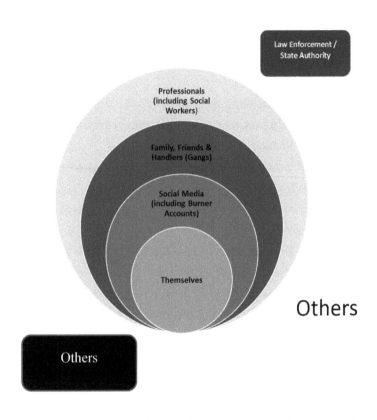

What was also interesting about the data was the indication that young people place a higher degree of trust in their interactions on social media than they do in their own family, friends and other physical social interactions. In explains this, most young people reported that there is a significant and common understanding of anonymity and openness on social media. This is especially true when it comes to young people having what is called burner social media accounts.

These burner accounts allow young people to connect to other like-minded young people and groups anonymously. Some connect for the obvious reasons of crime and criminality. Others connect for other reasons such as getting advice or highlighting ills in society that they are concerned or passionate about.

For some young people, who are part of the LGBT+ community but not comfortable with being open about their sexuality, burner accounts allow them some level of freedom in expressing themselves. They also use these burner accounts to set up meets with other persons, which is a dangerous practice within itself.

Overall, young people based their trust on loyalty and continuity. Anything else makes giving and earning trust a fleeting phenomenon with each stage having its own set of criteria. Further, the criteria are quite fragile and thus any breaches can see once trusted individuals move down to the less trusted paradigms. When this happens, moving back up into the higher trust brackets is difficult and, in some cases, quite impossible.

Chapter Seventeen – New Role Proposal

My new way of undertaking direct work with young people and the findings of my research on how young people trust and distribute their thrust changed my entire approach to social work. It also made me realise that there was a gap in social work for a new category of social workers. This new category of social workers, I thought, should focus on the new and creative ways of direct work and how to get more young people to be engaged with social workers and other professionals.

Far too many times I have seen how young people are categorised as 'hard to reach', 'non-engaging, 'difficult to deal with' or 'uninterested/displaying a lack of interest'. Once those terms are used against a young person, they are marked for the duration of any involvement by social services and professionals. Anyone who reads their files, before even contacting or meeting the young person, would automatically have a preconceived judgement of that young person.

My Team Managers and colleagues can tell you that throughout my social work journey so far, I always make it a point of going to meet a young person with an open mind and without any preconceived judgements. I would read the previous assessments and reports of course but would reserve my professional judgement until I had met the young person.

This was my way of making that first connection to the young person and start to build trust. In my opinion, the trust could not be built with that young person when there are already preconceived judgements about them.

To fill the gap in social work that I had identified, I spoke to my team manager and asked if I could submit a proposal for a new type of social worker. I explained to her that the vision I had was that there would eventually be a team of social workers who were skilled and had experience in devising creative ways to interact with and communicate with young people.

The remit of this team would be to take the cases involving young people that other social workers were having difficulties engaging with. The social workers would have to prove that they had genuinely tried everything within their power to engage with these young people.

My team manager agreed to my request and asked me to put together the proposal and presentation so that she could take it to the Service Manager for a discussion. I spent the next week working on the proposal and then sent it to my Team Manager. She scheduled a meeting with me so that I could brief her before she took it to the Service Manager.

In that meeting, after I had discussed the proposal, my team manager asked me to add an extra slide to the presentation listing the benefits to the young people and the Local Authority as a whole. I had already listed the benefits to the young people under the separate headings, but she wanted me to collate them in one place for maximum effect. Some of what was discussed are as follows:

1. Social workers with a specialist practice skill in mentoring.
2. Fewer referrals to external agencies. Young people prefer to speak to one named person rather than different people.
3. Fewer chances of cases being closed for lack of engagement, only to be re-referred within a few months or less.
4. Other social workers can be trained on the new strategies of direct work so that only the 'extreme cases' are sent to the new team.
5. Young people can take their time in opening up to social workers rather than be forced to open up by social workers working to timescales.

My team manager advised was onboard my proposal as she saw that there was an issue with getting young people to engage a need for this to be addressed. She sent the proposal to the Service Manager and scheduled a three-way meeting. In that meeting, the Service Manager also gave her approval to the proposal and invited me to a manager's meeting to pitch the proposal to all the Team Managers and Practice Consultants.

To say that I was nervous is an understatement but I held my nerve and delivered my pitch. There were lots of questions asked and clarification sought and I was prepared with the answers. At the end of my presentation, the Team Managers and Practice Consultants agreed to this new intervention and I was given the green light to put it into effect.

After the meeting, I spoke with the Service Manager and we agree on the parameters of the new role. In the initial phase, I would be the sole person in this role where I would lend my support to other social workers on their cases. I would hold case consultations with them, attend meetings with them, and in some instances, meet with their young person on their own. I would then provide written or verbal feedback to the social worker who would then add a case note to that young person's file.

After six months, the role and work undertaken would be revised. If there was evidence that the strategies and intervention methods used resulted in a significant increase in engagement of young people, the role would become permanent and a small team created around it. And that was how I became the first-ever Lead for Mentoring Young People, YOS, and Youth Violence for the Local Authority's Localities Teams.

Chapter Eighteen – Lead for Mentoring Young People

Being the Lead for Mentoring Young People, YOS and Youth Violence opened up a few doors for me and catapulted me to new heights in my career. I was allowed to deliver training and information sessions for international social workers and also hosted Zoom Q and A sessions for students and newly qualified social workers. Further, I was put forward to be a permanent member of the Resettlement and Aftercare Panel within the local authority.

This panel met monthly to devise action plans for young people who were about to be release from prison and who required that extra bit of support. At this panel, we considered accommodation for the young person, the continued involvement of services and professionals, and further support to the young person's extended family. Overall, the action plan devised by the Resettlement and Aftercare Panel was intended to reduce the risk of reoffending and to help the young person integrate back into society.

Another opportunity came when I answered an internal vacancy alert to join the Accelerated Support Team (AST) as a casual family support worker. In this role, I would work on some evenings and weekends making welfare calls and visits to young people and their families. I was also allocated to one young person as their named worker for me to work in collaboration with helping them and their families to deal with and manage any issues and concerns that were highlighted in the referral to our services.

With my new role and responsibilities, and my excellent case amazement (according to my Team Manager), I was being given more complex cases to oversee. My team manager once told me that I was her 'go-to' person when she had a new case and was unsure who to give it to. I was humbled by her faith and belief in me and readily took on any challenges she sent my way.

In addition to taking on more complex cases, my team manager also asked me to provide support and supervision to a final year student who had joined our team. Her Trainee Practice Educator was off sick for an extended period and my team manager said that I was the next best person to support and supervise her. I was also humbled when she mentioned that the new Service Manager agreed with her and approved of me supporting and supervising the student.

I decided to use this new opportunity as a way for me to see if I was ready to be a Practice Educator myself. Even though I had provided support to a previous student, and he was the first time that I was being asked to do so in an official capacity. I was not going to waste this opportunity.

Over the next few weeks, I met with the student, read through and highlighted corrections and amendments to her work, and also provided her with the best examples of the episodes she was required to complete. I helped her contact professionals, set up meetings, and joined in on telephone calls she had with families. I also provided regular updates to my team manager on the student's performance and the level I thought she was at in regards to the demands of working in a localities team.

In one case supervision, I did with the student, I went through the processes, procedures, and episode templates that she would need to follow and fill for each case she was allocated. I was shocked when she told me that her Practice Educator did not take her through this process when she first started. It made me understand why she was having a hard time understanding and getting used to the processes and timeframes.

This got me thinking and in my next case supervision with my Team Manager, I floated the idea that the localities team devise and draft a processed and procedures manual complete with blank templates and episodes. This would be specific to the localities team and then be given to new workers as part of the induction process. My team manager stated that she liked the idea and would discuss it with the Service Manager.

As we were now working from home due to the Coronavirus pandemic, it was understandable why the student was having a difficult time with the amount of work that had to be done per case. You see, she was on her own at home and did not have the comfort and reassurance of the team physically with her. And as you can imagine, learning to navigate a case management system remotely and on tour own can be quite a daunting task.

At the end of my tenure supporting and supervising the student, I was confident that I was ready for the first phase of the Practice Educator course and to embark on another chapter of my social work journey. It was also me two years since I had qualified as a social worker and with feedback, I was receiving regarding my case management, and the added responsibilities I was given, I also felt ready to progress on and become a senior social worker.

I took into consideration the fact that my team manager repeatedly said that since my ASYE, I was doing complex cases and court reports that would have ordinarily been assigned to a senior social worker. She also made mention of the way I had supported other members of the team, including senior social workers, and how I had readily accepted the challenge to supervise a final year student.

I drafted an email to my team manager to advise her that I intended to apply and submit a portfolio to the Progression Panel. This was for me to be considered for progression to a senior social worker within the team. At that time, there were a couple of vacancies within the team and my team manager made it clear that she would prefer to fill those positions with senior social workers. I was super excited and could not see any reason why I would not be given consideration for progression.

Chapter Nineteen – Ready for Progression

I began working on my portfolio for the Progression Panel which was scheduled to meet within a few months. For this portfolio, I had to complete a reflective essay in the form of a case study and get feedback from both professionals and clients. I also had to receive the support and backing of my Team Manager. I was confident that I would get her backing as she had previously told me that I was already performing at a Senior social worker level.

I asked my team manager for a meeting to discuss my plans and stated that as we were due to have personal supervision the following week, we can add that item to the agenda. I agreed and continued working on my portfolio so that as soon as I got her support, I could make any amendments and send them to her for her to complete her sections.

To be honest, I was so excited that I kept looking at the progression criteria and cross-mapping with what I'd already achieved. I was pleased to see that I had achieved all elements of the criteria already.

The day of the personal supervision meeting came, and after we discussed everything else, we turned to the issue of my progression. My team manager listened to me make my case for her support and agreed that she would support me. We then took a look at the profession criteria document together and cross-mapped it with what I had already done. This was looking good in my favour.

At the end of the meeting, my team manager stated that she would send an email to the person responsible for the Practice Educator course as she wanted to put me forward for the first phase. She said that as soon as they responded to her, she would let me know.

Further, my team manager said that she wanted to clarify if there were any time or length of service requirements before one can be presented at the panel for progression. I pointed out that it was not mentioned in the official progression documents so should it be a factor.

The following week, I got an email from my team manager with the minutes of our supervision meeting. There was no mention of the Progression Panel in the body of the email so I thought a decision had not been received as yet. I closed the email and continued working on the report I had opened. It was a couple of hours before I returned to the email and opened the attached so that I could save it in my supervision folder.

While reading through it, I was shocked to see that my team manager had recorded that she had spoken to the person responsible for the Practice Educator course and the decision was that I had to wait until two years post ASYE to be considered for the course. Also recorded, was an answer received from the Progression Panel coordinator stating that I also had to wait until two years post ASYE before I can be considered for progression.

My first thought was that these were not told to me or discussed during the personal supervision meeting so what were they recorded in the official minutes? Further, there was no mention of waiting two years post ASYE before one could request further training or request to be progressed. So why was I being told this now and most importantly, why was it in the minutes when it was not discussed?

I decided to write a letter to my team manager asking for an explanation and asking for the decision to refuse me further training and progression to be reviewed. In that letter, I listed all the work that I had been doing since my ASYE and how I met the criteria for progression. I stated that it was unfair for me to be expected to shoulder the responsibilities of a senior social worker, and yet be denied the opportunity to progress to the level of a senior social worker.

I followed up the letter with a personal email to my Team Manager. In it, I stated how disappointed I was in the fact the personal supervision meeting minutes had information on it that was not discussed during that meeting. I told her that I felt let down and unsupported by her. Especially since she agreed that I was performing at a senior social worker level and ready to be progressed.

Up to this day, I have not received a response to the letter or the personal email I sent. I was completely blanked. Then add insult to injury, just a few days after I sent the letter and the email, my team manager sent out a team email alerting us that they had interviewed and hired a senior social worker to join the team. That's when I made the decision to tender my resignation and continue my social work journey elsewhere.

Chapter Twenty – It Is Because I Am Black?

Being blatantly passed over for further training and progression made me angry. Especially when external persons were brought in to fill positions that internal staff could have been promoted to. Especially when some of these external persons were white, female, and qualified the same year as me or just a couple of years before me. Was I passed over because I was a black male social worker?

I was hoping that this was not the case, but the more I thought about it, the more it seemed that way and I was bothered by it. Added to that, the fact that my team manager had not even acknowledged or responded to my letter and personal email suggested that there was more going on that I was unaware of. It certainly could not be because I was not two years post ASYE. I was a couple of months shy of being two years post qualified. Further, I thought it was unfair also to discount my ASYE.

I followed up my letter and email with other emails and calls to my team manager until I was able to speak with her. I asked her why I was being refused further training and progression. Her exact words to me were, "Aleski, I tried, but the powers that be have the final say and it's out of my hands."

I asked who she was referring to and she refused to say. However, she made it a point to highlight the fact that she had passed my requests on to the relevant persons and the answer received was no.

I had heard stories of other black male social workers being passed over for promotion and actively kept from accessing further training. However, I didn't think it would happen to me. I don't know what made me think otherwise. Maybe it was because, in my mind, I had proven myself and my worth to my team manager and service managers. I had been with the Local Authority since my very first placement and I thought that should count for something.

Further, I had also written my university dissertation on this very subject. You would have remembered I mentioned it in one of the earlier chapters. My dissertation was on the challenges and experiences of black male social workers in the Children and Young People Service. Coincidently, my dissertation and the subsequent piece I wrote for the Professional social work magazine, was widely shared within the local authority.

My research found that black male social workers were often side-lined in the workplace and their worth was undervalued. They were stereotyped by both colleagues and clients alike and judged prematurely. Black male social workers were also pigeonholed with the types of cases they were allocated My research found that they were always given the cases involving black young people and their families. They were also given cases that no other social worker wanted.

My research also found that black male social workers had their work overtly and unfairly scrutinised and had to work twice to prove themselves. Their requests for training and promotion were more likely to be denied or delayed as compared to their non-black counterparts. This is why, according to the findings of my research, it was difficult to persuade young black me to become social workers.

"Now, if the challenges and experiences mentioned above are for men in general then one can only imagine how it will be for black male social workers who have the added scrutiny on them due to their ethnicity and gender. One can even argue that the challenges and experiences faced by black male social workers are vastly different compared to that of their white counterparts.

The same stereotypical and racist connotations attributed to black service users are also attributed to black male social workers. Further, black male social workers are often typecast in regards to the cases they are allocated and the service users they work with.

Social workers interviewed stated that they were given the cases involving gangs and 'problematic and difficult' families. Some even said that the service users they were allocated were all black or of ethnic minority backgrounds. This not only hampered their development but also limits them demonstrating their potential as social workers." (Brandy-Williams, 2019)

It was not lost on me that the very thinking that I had researched was now happening to me. Here I was, a black male social worker being denied progression and further training. Here I was, a black male social worker having to challenge the system and fight against what I believed were unfair practices being used to justify denying me progression and further training.

I had come full circle from researching the challenges and experiences of black male social workers to being a black male social worker experiencing those challenges.

Chapter Twenty-One – Black Men in Social Work

In this chapter, I will share some excerpts, including some of the findings from my dissertation directly from the final version submitted to my university. I am proud to say that I received a First-Class grade for my dissertation research project.

Information received from the HCPC confirms that there is already a low percentage of male social workers and this is since there are some negative assumptions in social work surrounding the issue of men working and having a career in Social Work. These assumptions can stem from the underlying reasons why a male would want to have a career in a female-dominated sector to questions on the sexuality and sexual orientation of males working in social services and as social workers.

For a black man, in addition to these assumptions and questions, there are also the stereotypical issues and concerns over the effectiveness and viability of him being a social worker. Stereotypes of drugs, gangs, and violence are automatically attributed to young black men and for these young black men to pursue a career as a social workers, questions are asked about whether or not these stereotypical assumptions can be shaken or even avoided.

Then there is the insinuation that these young men must have had some traumatic experience in their lives at a young age which landed them on the path to becoming social workers – an assumption that is not usually made about non-black young men choosing a career pathway into social services and social work.

On the other hand, some would see young black men entering the social services sector as social workers as a positive thing. They would be able to relate more to service users who are from black, Asian and other minority ethnicities and perhaps offer more suitable, productive and effective interventions.

However, the desire and lack of motivation for young black men to become social workers have been the subject of many debates, conversations, and research. There have been many theories as to why this is including differential educational achievement, overt and covert discrimination and oppression, and even the lack of career progression as a social worker (Mbarushimana & Robbins, 2015).

Then there have been many reports from black social workers about the experiences and challenges they have faced working in social services, such as lack of training and support. Those accounts have dissuaded many young black men from becoming social workers as they would not want to go through the same experiences and challenges that already qualified and established social workers go through, especially being a target for racism.

Racist attitudes and unrealistic expectations of black social workers do not only come from within the workplace but also from the services users that they interact with. Black service users usually expect the black social workers to understand their issues and problems and side with them in any decisions or interventions.

Black service users also expect that black social workers can be that metaphorical bridge between themselves and the white oppressive and racist institutions that social services and social workers belong to. Some black service users even go as far as to accuse the black social workers of being agents of oppressive practice against them and in service to the white establishments.

Once the black social worker challenges what the service user says, it can lead to a conflict of loyalties and a breakdown in the trust and relationship the service user had begun to develop with the social worker. The conflict of loyalties experienced by the black social worker can also lead to a struggle between the power that they have a social worker, and how inferior they are made to feel by the treatment and attitudes of not just the service user but the mechanisms of the organisation they represent and are a part of.

Black male social workers are on the one hand celebrated and sought after, and on the other hand, they are portrayed in a negative light. All the academic writings and publications perused all agree that there is a growing need for black male social workers. They can be positive role models and service users, especially other young black males, will be able to relate to them and aspire to be like them.

Black male social workers can also pose a direct challenge to the view that black men need to continue to embrace the hyper-masculinity of social norms and engage in activities that are illegal and could land them in prison. These same young black men can simultaneously contend with their masculinity and still be able to perform in a female-dominated sector, without having to compromise and without having their masculinity questioned or their sexuality assumed.

There is a need for social services as a whole to be more culturally diverse, from the top echelon of management down to the workers on the front line. Black social workers need to feel represented. And, with that representation be offered the support that they are currently lacking from within the profession. Overall, the profession as it stands, needs to be sensitised to the experiences and challenges of black male social workers, based off of their lived experiences and not based on assumptions, attitudes and biased stereotypes.

Chapter Twenty – Two – Research Findings Part One

Assumptions, Stereotypes & Typecasting

According to Billson (2018), young black men are stereotyped constantly and this added with the negative portrayal and assumptions about them creates a problematic and challenging journey from youth to adulthood and even throughout their careers and professional lives. This difficult journey not only limits their development and growth but also affects their self-belief, determination, and morale. This argument is echoed by all of the black male social workers who were interviewed for this research project. One of them who has been allocated the moniker of Alex had this to say:

In all walks of life, black men are stereotyped and judged so it's obvious that even at work this will continue.

This view was a repeat occurrence throughout the interviews as the black male social workers spoke on the many assumptions and stereotypes being made about them by service users, colleagues, and professionals in the industry. They argued that due to the fact that they were black and male it was assumed that they would be best suited to work with families and young people who are involved in gang culture, drugs, and aspects of crime and criminal activity. This also feeds into the narrative where black young men are stereotyped as deviant in addition to being more susceptible to crime – both as victim and perpetrator – than anyone else (Piquero, 2015).

According to the interviewees, even the service users they work with or the parents of the young people allocated, viewed them in this negative manner and as a result were resistant to engaging with them and some even went as far as requesting a different social worker. Social Worker JohnJay gave an example where a young person who had gotten into trouble for being involved with smoking and selling drugs where the young person assumed that because he was a young black male that he indulged in that activity and pastime. JohnJay recollected that the young person:

...looked at me side-eye as if to say c'mon you've done this before haven't you?

JohnJay surmises that this is another factor where some service users assume that because you are of the same gender and ethnicity as them and also close in age, you will be more accepting of their behaviour and as a result be more lenient in intervening. Mbarushimana & Robbins (2015) made mention of this in their research and argued that service users sharing the same culture, ethnicity, and background as social workers sometimes have an expectation of preferential justification and acceptance.

On the other hand, interviewee Clive has a different view and approach to dealing with service users who think that because he is a young black male similar to them that he would somehow be lenient and more accepting of their behaviour. Clive says that tells them that even though he understands what they are going through as he has faced some of the same hurdles as them, ultimately, he is there to do his job and to do it well.

"I'm also going through the same struggles and have to jump through the same hurdles that you do BUT I'm here to do a job but don't take me for a fool…"

Interviewee Bill also supports Clive's stance in showing understanding to the service user's situation while at the same time setting boundaries and remaining professional so that the assumptions that the service user makes are proven wrong. Bill remarks that when you show understanding and still stick your principles:

The young people not only respect you more but are now more willing to talk to you and take advice. They even start seeing you as a positive role model.

Even though the young black male social workers are seen as positive role models, there remains an assumption about their motives for entering the profession and also about their sexuality. While none of the social workers who were interviewed disclosed anything about having their sexuality and motives questioned, they however were aware of the stigma surrounding the sexuality of male social workers in general.

Interviewees JohnJay, Bill, Joseph and Clive all agreed that assumptions about the sexuality of male social workers and being perceived as gay prevents more males, especially black males, from joining the profession. Further, it raises further questions about the reason men become social workers.

Kosberg (2002) argues that social work literature often portrays men in social work as being gay while Hall (2010) states that men, in general, are seeing as sexual predators, dangerous to children, and portrayed as having sexual ulterior motives in becoming social workers. Here is what the social workers interviewed had to say:

It's been said that many young men that enter social work are gay because social work historically has been a female profession, and, *...men that go into it tend to be gay. (Clive)*

It's sad that there is still that stereotype and assumption that male social workers are gay as it stops more young black men from becoming social workers as black men care more about being called gay than others. (Bill)

Yea that's what everyone says that male social workers are gay and that's just stupid. (Joseph)

Due to these assumptions about male social workers being gay or sexual predators (Gillingham, 2006), interviewee JohnJay says that he has had to develop ways in which to guard himself against any allegations or complaints of sexual inappropriateness such as leaving doors open when speaking with young female service users or side hugging them or not hugging them at all.

Warde (2009) in supporting what JohnJay says, contends that male social workers have had to develop strategies in their day-to-day practice and interventions to guard against allegations and complaints.

However, interviewee Clive also countered by stating there is:

...a big change now because you've got a lot of males who are heterosexual and are actually going into the job because that is what they really want to do.

Career Progression, Support & Respect

Brown & Jones (2004) argue that as a direct result of the assumptions on the sexuality of male social workers, those who enter the profession do so with the sole aim of advancing quickly into the upper echelons of management and this is to avoid any allegations of misconduct or inappropriate sexual impropriety. Lupton (2006) further stated that when male social workers ascend to positions of management, they do so more rapidly than their female counterparts and according to Lewis (2004) this is in keeping with the social gender norms of men being in positions of power and management. Interviewee Clive thinks that while this may be true for men in general, as a black man in social work this is not the same. Clive says:

Men may get to the top quicker but black men for some reason don't. There are no black male team managers...as you go higher up, it becomes whiter.

Then when asked if there is enough of a progress route for black male social workers, Clive had this to say:

I don't think there's an effective path for black males to make their way through the social work system and progress quickly enough. A black male progressing in the world is a threat. Not all white people have that view but white people, in general, don't want to see black people progress. And I feel a black man at the top will shatter the reality of what is out there in the streets. And that's why I'm so driven in wanting to break through that glass ceiling.

Further on in the interview, when Clive was asked about the most challenging thing, he has faced about being a young black male social worker he replied:

Progression has been a challenge to some degree… I know a lot of individuals who make decisions about me based on the fact I'm a young black male and haven't got the life experience for progression.

The challenges associated with progression are not the only challenge that the young black male social workers interviewed have to deal with as they also mentioned the fact that they are not supported or even respected among their peers and among service users. Alex says there is a lack of respect for him as a black male social worker and his abilities are sometimes second-guessed and questioned. Bob thinks that there is a lack of training and support for him as a black male social worker especially in how to handle cases where domestic violence is an issue and a concern. He articulates that:

I remember having to deal with a service user who was a victim of DV and I had no support or anything. I didn't know what to say to how to go about showing empathy. A male social worker was probably the last person she wanted to see at that moment.

Not only is there no support but there is also a lack of respect and according to interviewee Bill it sometimes comes from his peers and although most times it is unspoken, it is obvious to see from their actions and reactions.

My gosh you get to see the politics and when you're in the staff room you see the different clicks...and they look at me like look there's the black guy and he's got a mohawk...they may not be saying it out loud but I feel the energy and the vibe...

Revans (2003) argues that once black and minority social workers are recruited then they are left to feel like they are unsupported and many don't receive adequate or additional training and thus are unable to respond to the needs of service users and intervene appropriately on their behalf. Goldstein (2002) agrees and added that black and minority social workers feel disrespected when they have their abilities and capabilities questioned, and the service and interventions they carry out with service users scrutinised by white counterparts and managers as this is a form of covert racism (Brockmann et al, 2001).

Celebrated or discriminated?

Even though the black and minority social workers have their work closely monitored and assessed (Goldstein, 2002), according to research done by Mbarushimana & Robbins (2015), black and minority social workers still feel that they have to work twice as hard just to feel appreciated and worthwhile. McLaughlin (2012) argues that there is a level of institutionalised racism existing in Social Services affecting black and minority social workers where white workers and management are the dominant social group. This is exacerbated by the fact that some black and minority social workers are recruited simply to deal with and work with families and service users deemed as problematic (Singh, 1992).

Two of the social workers interviewed for this research project shares this view that an element of indirect racism towards them existed in the cases they were allocated, the way they were treated by colleagues and management, and the atmosphere and environment of the office. Interviewee JohnJay queried that he:

...kept thinking why was I only getting cases with black service users who were either difficult to work with or live-in black areas? I mean at least give me another type of case to see what I am capable of and not restrict me to just black cases and black service users.

When asked if his gender and ethnicity play a role in the types of cases and services users he was allocated, interviewee Clive was quite clear in his response when he said:

It does because initially when I first started my local authority role, all the gang cases I got being a young, black, and male…you fit that stereotype and that's why (they're) always giving them to you…

The racial bias and stereotypes do not only relate to the office but also relate to other professionals and services that black male social workers work in partnership with and this, in turn, creates a hostile and tense situation (Storry & Childs, 2002). social worker Clive recalls an incident with the police below:

Even outside of work I get stopped by the police. I might be doing a home visit, and the police will be wondering what I'm doing until I show them the badge. Stereotypes are still apparent whether I wear a badge of a social worker or not. It's something I have to deal with. Those barriers whether in the professional world or personal are always going to be there.

Clive also said that racist attitudes and behaviours can also come from black service users towards black social workers as he explains some service users sees him as a:

…black man being used by a white system. You are in other words a coconut (black on the outside, white on the inside) because…you are working for the system and against us.

Fortunately, it is not at all times that black male social workers or black social workers, in general, are discriminated against or endure racism but are celebrated and appreciated as according to Chand (2008), black service users see black social workers as bridging the gap between them and the white establishments. According to interviewees JohnJay and Clive, black service users identify with them on a level that they don't experience with other service users and thus they are able to not just build relationships but also implement successful interventions.

The client group, the young people take to me very well. I think being a young black male helps because I can identify with them on the same level...I do talk slang with them, I speak on the same level. Then they understand that he's kinda like me then...that's how I break through the barrier with them. (Clive)

Most service users are happy when they see someone like them working on their behalf you know, it makes them feel represented and that they would listen to... (Clive)

Epilogue – The Journey Continues

Since the day I decided to undertake postgraduate studies in social work, my journey can be compared to an ocean current. At one point, it is smooth, free-flowing, and calm.

Then at another point, it is turbulent, unpredictable, and can pull you beneath the surface. However, as a social worker, I compare myself to a professional swimmer who is able to navigate the currents and stay afloat.

The journey I have been through, from student social worker to qualified social worker, had the potential to end my journey prematurely and indefinitely. However, even though there were times I wanted to give up, I persevered and made it to the end.

Along the way, I've been supported and encouraged by people who I saw as guardian angels and mentors. They kept me motivated and focused.

I started my journey with passion, and I still have that same today. A passion to help young people and their families have the best outcomes through bespoke and targeted interventions.

A passion to support and train the next generation of empathetic and purpose-driven social workers. A passion to make social work more inclusive, diverse and less of an enigma.

Throughout my journey, I have been able to convert my unfettered zest to make a difference in the lives of children and young people, into a holistic and measured approach. This allows me to help families to use their collective strengths to achieve better and more sustained outcomes.

I have learnt along the way that it's not about what I can do for families as a social worker, it's about what I can support families in doing for themselves. It is about making a difference.

However, I have also realised that as a social worker, if I don't take the time to look after myself, I won't be able to give my best self to the children, young people and families that I work with. I ensure that I take the time out to evaluate, regulate and re-energise myself.

In doing so, I can be the kind of social worker to families as I would want a social worker to be to me. This, I think is key to successful outcomes.

My outcome for myself is that I never lose my passion for social work. In fact, I hope that it grows and flourishes along my continued journey. I am not where I want to be as yet, but I am determined to get there.